Enjoy the feast. Take care. Stay healthy. Love Leah 2016

Leah's Raw Food Feast

Recipes & Advice For 9 Days Of Fantastic Raw Living

By Leah Salmon
The Naturally You Coach

Published 2013

By Leah Salmon
The Naturally You Coach
83 Wentworth House, High Street North, Dunstable, Beds

Whilst every effort has been made to ensure that the information contained in this book is accurate and up to date, it is advisory only and should not be used as an alternative to seeking qualified professional advice. The author and publisher cannot be held responsible for actions or omissions that may be taken by the reader as a result of reliance on the information contained in this book. The information is taken entirely at the reader's own risk.

Some recipes in this book contain nuts and/or seeds

10 9 8 7 6 5 4 3

ISBN 9780 9926 4221 1

Author: Leah Salmon
Cover Design: Jeremy Salmon www.wedesign.media

Printed In England

What are people saying about Leah's Raw Food Feast…

"I love this book! It gives great information and so many good, tasty recipes using ingredients that can be easily sourced.   I like that the whole book has an under tone of "I can do it, so you can too" kind of feel. Lovely book!!!"

International Vegan TV Cook & Author Kirly Sue of KirlySuesKitchen.co.uk

"Leah's Raw Food Feast is a must have for anyone who wants to incorporate more raw food into their everyday lifestyle. It's packed with loads of delicious but simple recipes, nutritional info, helpful transition tips and mouth-watering photos. My all time favourite recipe is the legendary Mango Pie, which is so easy to make, and goes down a storm with everyone. I also love that Leah lives by her word and has an absolutely amazing healing energy that emanates from her and her whole(some) family."

Debrose Searchwell, Founder of Natural November, Raw Food Chef & Expert & Owner of LibRaw Foods

"Leah's so passionate about what she does and it shows in her recipes and work. She managed to get my family to love green smoothies, mango pie and kale salad without us feeling pressured into being healthy and her recipe for hot sauce is the best I've ever tasted."

Julian Hall The Ultrapreneur Founder of UltraKids.Club and UltraAcademy.org.uk

"I was thrilled to find out Leah was revising the Raw Food Feast Book! I do a juice cleanse once a month and find that eating raw is the best way to ease myself back into food. Leah's Raw Food Feast helps me do this and is packed with delicious ideas for meals and snacks to have anytime of day - the avocado fries & cinnamon apple chips with salted caramel sauce are my favourites!"

Merissa Hamilton, Owner of Naturally Simple Hair Care, Duafe Galleria & Sankofa Creative Co, mother of 2

Thanks to...

This book is dedicated to all the delicious raw foods that made it easy for me to love my raw days, you lovelies are great!!!

Mangos & Watermelon – Two of the most delicious fruits the most high ever graced this planet with, you are simply delicious, you need no accompaniment (except a bib and a bowl), I love and appreciate you.

Tahini & Carob Milk (page 39) – This little lifesaver introduced me to raw carob and it's sweet rich taste. Even though I can't stomach tahini on it's own, you transform my smoothies and sauces. Thanks to Jingee & Storm Talifero from The Garden Diet for inspiring this drink.

Kale Salad & Fried Mushrooms (pages 75 & 67) - Once I decide to really go for it with raw food, it took me a night of watching Karen Knowler YouTube videos and a quick shopping trip the next day to seal the deal. I hadn't even heard of kale before her video and mushrooms seldom entered my diet, but since then, these 2 simple foods make my raw food days filling and satisfying. Thank you so much Karen.

Tomato & Buckwheat Bread (page 64) - It didn't take me long to realise that one food I missed most on my raw days is bread and dry savoury foods. After many disappointing and failed attempts (I'm not a big fan of flaxseed which is my main dilemma), a slight adaptation of the buckwheat pizza base from The Sunny Raw Kitchen's recipe ebook, put the biggest smile of relief on my face. Thanks Sunny Raw Kitchen.

Green Smoothies (page 35) - The easiest, tastiest way to get loads of green goodness into your diet and it's a real hit with even the fussiest children. Drinking them always makes me feel like I'm drinking a whole field of nature's finest, sunlight, clouds, summer breeze and all.

Tropical Cheesecake (page 105) – You well and truly restored my faith in raw vegan cakes, many of which I find too rich and a poor alternative to the creaminess of dairy.

Pink Ice Cream (page 98) - This simplified version of Karen Knowler's Raspberry Passion Pudding, is easily one of my favourite breakfasts on a warm day, meals on "feeling a little peckish" days and desserts, on the rare occasion we have them after a meal. Three ingredients, 1 big hit of fruit love.

Avocado Fries (page 66) – The versatility of this humble pear never ceases to amaze me. It's a great addition to a salad, it creates a delicious chocolate pudding and now it transforms into a French fry replacement that is crisp on the outside, soft and slightly warm on the inside and just delicious all the way through. An absolute favourite with everyone in our house.

Agave Nectar & Raw Chocolate Powder – Both of you have received criticism and praise in equal measure, but both of you made the transitioning times for many raw foodies possible, so thanks for playing your part in the revolution

"Raw Food Is More Than Salads & Carrot Sticks, It's About Getting A Natural Energy Fix"

Leah Salmon

Contents

Main Meals

Desserts

Top: Cinnamon Apple Chips & Salted Caramel from page 114
Bottom: Kale, Mango & Tomato Salad from page 75

"Hi and Welcome To My Raw Week, Well, '9 Day Week' But Who's Counting!!!"

The aim of this book is:

- To help you add more fresh live and raw foods to your life.

- To provide simple plans that are easy and realistic for you to follow, no matter how much or how little time you have.

- To help you take your raw food experience as quickly or slowly as you want.

- To help you commit to going raw for just 3, 5 or 9 days.

- To provide healthy nutrient rich drink, dessert, breakfast, main course and snack recipes you'll love.

- To show you how great you can feel after spending just a short amount of time with more live food in your life.

- To make the experience fun filled, delicious and smooth sailing

My Raw Food Journey

I was a nutritionist for a few years before I discovered the raw food diet. The type who thought I knew it all already!!!

At that time I was already sending out my Naturally You newsletter and I would often get feedback from the subscribers. But in the space of a few weeks, I had 3 people send me a link to the same website on raw food which was www.thegardendiet.com. I had a quick look and it looked interesting, The pictures of all the fresh fruit looked lovely, but it just seemed extreme and a little strange so I quickly moved on.

Then the world of health started to pick up on raw foods more and I started seeing it crop up more in forums and newsletters I read.

At this time, I was a piscetarian (mainly vegetarian but ate fish, no meat or poultry), I had good energy, but I knew things could be better. In my business, I was selling a lot of products, herbs, nutritional oils, supplements and green powders. I took most of the things I sold, but it didn't always feel right to have to take so many processed things (as natural as they were) to maintain health, my focus was sometimes less on my foods and more on making sure I supplemented regularly with the products that I sold.

When I had tables at events, seminars or spoke to people over the phone and email about their health, so many of them were happy to keep eating the way they were and just wanted to buy herbs and supplements to patch themselves up, like a quick fix.

This never sat well with me and it began to feel like I was possibly doing more harm than good by not pushing people to look at their foods more. I'd just give in and sell them the quick fix they were after.

This uneasy feeling didn't last too long thankfully.

I'd known about Metabolic Typing for some time, which is a process you use to find out what the best balance of nutrients is for your particular body type using an in depth questionnaire and I finally decided to get certified as a Metabolic Typing Advisor.

At this point I stopped selling all products and felt like I'd found my true calling in life; teaching people how to use their foods, instead of drugs, chemicals and surgeries, to improve their health, using a proven system of finding the foods that suit someone's individual biochemistry, helping them create a meal plan around it and giving them continual coaching and support to ensure they stuck to and benefited from it all.

One of the founders of the concept of metabolic typing was Dr Weston Price. In short, he was a dentist who wanted to find out why people in the western world had so many dental problems and why indigenous people rarely suffered from dental problems or other degenerative diseases.

(Left: Indigenous Eskimos & Right: Aborigines)

In order to discover why, he travelled to 14 indigenous tribes, from the Inuit Eskimos to the Ugandans in Africa and studied their lives. Even though their diets were all very different from one another (in some cases, completely opposite), there were a few things that he found in common with all of them:

- They ate no refined or devitalised foods
- Sweets, even natural sweets were used very rarely
- All food was organic, seasonal and eaten freely
- They enjoyed regular physical exercise and periods of fasting
- They got plenty of unpolluted air and clean water
- They had virtually NO cavities, degenerative diseases or emotional issues
- Most interestingly was that a lot of their foods were eaten raw or very lightly cooked.

So yet again I was brought face to face with the 'Raw Food Thing' and decided now was the time to take a much closer look at it.

I went off and bought all the eBooks from The Garden Diet site, downloaded loads of other recipes and started to add more and more raw meals and snacks into our life. I was married and our first child was still a baby at the time, so quick juices and big salads along with our meals made up the bulk of our raw food life.

I bought a dehydrator and all I had at the time were 2 recipes for raw vegan sweets, fruit leathers and garlic chips, so after a few weeks I got bored and packed it away (I actually almost sent it back, luckily I didn't).

Even though I had plenty of recipes, I began to find it difficult to piece all the meals together into some kind of logical order, to form something resembling a meal plan.

I was scared to go raw for a whole day because I didn't know what to eat to keep me full enough.

I'd been eating a cooked diet my whole life, I had no idea what a raw vegan could possibly survive on, even for one day,

I really wanted to do it but I was really stumped on how.

It sounds really silly reading this back, it was just one day, I'd fasted for a whole day before so what's the big deal in just eating foods that hadn't been cooked, right?!? Well there were 2 saving graces that found me and showed me the way.

I read an email from a raw foodist's mailing list I was subscribed to and she simply shared what she'd eaten for a day. Eureka!!!

That was it, finally the answer I'd been looking for, what someone ate in a day of being raw vegan. From this I could see how simple it would be to plan a meal for a day and I was on a mission to create my food plan, similar to what I had seen, but more to my taste.

Soon after this and after reading and studying and compiling recipes, I started searching YouTube for inspiration (and there was a bag of it on there), when I stumbled across a set of recipe demonstrations by Karen Knowler, The Raw Food Coach. They were for Fried Mushrooms (find my version on page 67), Kale & Avocado salad (find my version on page 75), Almond Milk (find my version on page 38), Nori Rolls (find my version on page 91) and Muesli (find my version on page 50). I then stumbled upon Shazzie's Mushroom & Walnut Burgers recipe.

That was it!!!! I decided to go raw. I had a basic plan and the motivation, I was set.

The next day I went shopping, got everything I needed and started preparing things that night.

The next day, I successfully spent the day as a raw vegan, and the next day, and the next day and the day after that too. I stayed 100% raw for 5 days, it was fantastic. That's when I decided to start doing a week a month like this.

But there was one little (well pretty big actually) problem I was facing....

My work as a Metabolic Typing Advisor was to show people the foods that worked for them and then to help them build a meal plan around it as I know there isn't one diet that suits everyone. I am a Slow Oxidiser, one of the carbohydrate types and as such, need to have higher levels of carbohydrates, rather than fats and proteins to function optimally (which means you feel great, not just ok when people ask you how you are!!!)

For some reason though, I was convinced, probably because of all the less supportive information I'd read on raw foods and the vegan and vegetarian diet, that I **needed** to make sure I ate loads of fatty, high protein, high purine (a type of protein) foods as a raw vegan, because the vegan and raw vegan diets are apparently seriously lacking in them.

So the first few days of my raw food weeks would be great, but then I would start to get really tired, crave bread and sweets, feel really unsatisfied no matter how much I ate and longed to go back to cooked foods again.

So what was I eating you ask? Loads of fatty protein rich raw foods!!! Big mistake for my body type.

Typically in a day I'd have:

Breakfast	A thick almond milk with hemp protein powder and Udo's nutritional oil
Snack	A handful of nuts and some fresh fruit
Lunch	A salad with lots of olive oil, avocado, nut mayo, mushrooms, raw bread and sprouts
Afternoon snack	A raw dessert like date and nut sweets, raw chocolates or cashew ice cream
Dinner	Nori rolls with more avocado or walnut and mushroom burgers on kale avocado salad

All lovely foods, but just not right for me.

"One Size Fits All Clothes & Diets Can Both Make You Look Fat And Feel Like Crap"
Leah Salmon

While eating a cooked diet, I may have had a few cravings but at least I felt happy, energetic, fulfilled and emotionally stable, because I was eating many cooked wholesome foods for my type. There were many times on raw food that this wasn't the case.

I felt like Victoria Butenko (author of the very popular Green Smoothie Revolution Book), when after years of success on raw foods, her health started declining and she didn't know what to do. Her answer was dark green leafy vegetables and green smoothies, mine was Metabolic Typing.

When the penny finally dropped and I married my raw vegan life with my Metabolic Typing requirements, that's when, during my 4th pregnancy (a difficult time to mentally and emotionally commit to anything), I managed to stay 100% raw vegan for 30 days.

During that time, my new metabolically typed raw vegan days looked a bit more like this

Breakfast	A green smoothie (spinach orange and banana typically)
Lunch	A salad with lots of romaine lettuce, tomatoes, cucumbers, radishes, kale, carrots and small portions of buckwheat pizza bread or eggless egg salad
Afternoon snack	A tahini milk or green juice, but I didn't always need a snack as I did before
Dinner	A big leafy green salad, sprouts, tomatoes, avocado, nut mayo & coleslaw.

Even since then my needs have changed and I need far less fruit to feel satisfied, but big daily salads are still definitely for me.

If you have ever experienced a feeling of a lack of satisfaction from a supposedly wholesome healthy diet, consider discovering your Metabolic Type and when you have, you can adapt your meals around them.

Now let's get into the nitty gritty of raw foods, so you can get started on your journey

What Are Raw Foods?

Raw foods are natural whole foods that haven't been heated above 38°C / 105°F. Above this temperature, chemical changes take place within foods which, depending on how much higher the temperature gets, can destroy the enzymes, vitamins, some minerals, phytonutrients and other nutrients.

Raw foods (depending on the type) are a good source of water, vitamins, minerals and live enzymes.

Many raw foods are still in their living (or live) state (which means they are still growing & ripening), which makes them even more potent, sprouts being a prime example of a live raw food.

The obvious opposite of raw foods is cooked foods, so.....

Cooked foods are food which have been heated or processed in a way that exposes them to heats well over 38°C, which as stated above can sometimes cause harmful chemicals to be created and change the chemical composition of that food, so it's far from what it was originally. However, cooked foods aren't all evil and toxic and many cooked foods are very healthy for you.

How do we know that cooking can chemically alter a food?

If you test the nutrient levels of foods in their raw state compared to their cooked state, you will very often see a difference. Occasionally their mineral content will slightly increase, however their vitamin content will always significantly decrease

For example:

Vitamin C content	Broccoli 1 cup	Kale 1 cup	Carrot 1 cup
Cooked	64mg	53mg	5.6mg
Raw	89.2mg	80mg	7.6mg
Source: www.nutritiondata.com			

You will however find foods that have increases in their nutrient levels from cooking and there are some foods which are **unsafe** to eat raw, like kidney beans and white potatoes, so please also bear this in mind.

Possibly the most important things that are destroyed during cooking are the enzymes, which are largely responsible for the energy boost many people experience on raw foods.

You've mentioned enzymes a few times, are they really THAT important?

Without enzymes, life could literally not take place! Big claim I know, but they are the catalyst or driving forces behind many chemical reactions in the body, which produce the life sustaining mechanisms that keep us going.

Here are just some of the many functions enzymes carry out (I say many, but there are actually hundreds of actions they are responsible for):

- ✓ Digesting food to a size capable of being absorbed into the blood
- ✓ Rebuilding food into tissue of muscle, bone, organs, glands, etc.
- ✓ Working to store food in the liver and muscles for fuel later on
- ✓ Coagulating blood
- ✓ Attaching iron to red blood cells
- ✓ Eliminating carbon dioxide from the lungs
- ✓ Promoting oxidation
- ✓ Attacking waste material in the blood and preparing it for elimination
- ✓ Changing proteins into sugar or fat
- ✓ Changing carbohydrates into fat
- ✓ Changing fats into carbohydrate

So basically, even if you have good levels of proteins, fats, carbohydrates, amino acids etc in your body, without adequate levels of enzymes, you will find it difficult to make use of them.

We are born with a limited amount of enzymes, so they are found naturally in our bodies, but they don't last particularly long. So it's important to get a regular supply of them. They are virtually all destroyed during cooking and most food processing methods, which is why it is vital to get topped up regularly from live foods and if necessary, natural supplements.

So in conclusion, you'd be doing yourself a massive favour by adding more raw, live and enzyme rich foods to your life.

What's The Big Deal With Eating Raw foods Anyway?

There is one point I feel I need to stress at this point.

Food is essentially food

Why does it matter so much to people whether it's cooked or not?

There is a tendency in this society to over complicate things (especially where money is involved) when nature makes things very easy for us.

We are so accustomed to eating a mainly cooked food diet, that the thought of eating more raw foods can sometimes be what makes it seem like such a big leap, when it really isn't in many ways. If your diet is currently made up of mainly cheap processed foods, then increasing the fruits, vegetables, raw nuts, seeds and whole grains will be the first step.

But if you already have many of these things in your diet, having a few of them raw instead of cooked once in a while, is the next simple step.

If you put too much thought around it, it can definitely make this natural transition more difficult than it needs to be, which could prevent you from experiencing the real benefits you can get from it.

Hopefully the FAQ's (Frequently Asked Questions) next will help put your mind at ease further before we get to the really good stuff, the recipes!!!

FAQ's On Raw Foods

Here are some of the questions that I get asked most frequently about raw foods and a few I personally had when I started my journey.

Are they going to fill me up?
If a burger and chips, which has hardly any nutrition whatsoever, can be considered a proper filling meal, then kale & tomato salad with mushrooms & avocados can definitely leave you satisfied.

Once you know the foods that best suit your body type using Metabolic Typing or experimentation, it's easier to determine which foods will do a better job of satisfying you. At the very least, the higher levels of water and fibre raw foods typically contain will keep your appetite at bay for a few hours at least. Just eat until you are satisfied, and definitely don't worry about portion control or calorie counting.

Can I get enough nutrition out of them to keep me going?
As long as your digestive system is in good working order and you're chewing your foods properly, you are likely to get more nutrition from raw foods than cooked foods, because they are in their whole natural state, so your body is more likely to be able to digest them and get the abundant level of nutrients from them, especially if you find the foods that work best for you.

However, whether you are eating cooked or raw foods, if you have a clogged up colon, full of stuck on sludge and faecal matter, you are going to have a hard time getting the nutrients out of **anything** you eat. The water, fibre and nutrients found in raw foods will help your body to gently cleanse itself, but a more powerful colon cleanse before you start will do wonders for your body's ability to absorb the nutrients in your food.

Do I need the skill and knowledge of a qualified raw food chef to be able to make the foods properly?

You didn't need a qualification to make your cooked breakfast, lunch and dinner yesterday and you certainly don't need anything more than a chopping board and a blender in many cases, to make most of the meals in this book and in general.

Won't I get cold eating only raw foods

This is a very valid concern of many and it was my absolute fear before I started because I hate being cold!!! However, what I found was that my meagre level of physical exercise had much more to do with how my body produced heat than what I was eating.

In fact, I probably got colder eating a poor diet of hot cooked food than when I was eating higher quality raw foods. If you intend on having ice cold juice and salads in the height of a snow storm then you can expect to get cold and off balance quickly, and I'd never recommend you eat too many foods or drinks straight from the fridge anyway, especially in colder weather, as this can also drop your body temperature too much. Eat warming raw foods in cold weather (like foods containing pepper, cinnamon, ginger etc) and the more water rich ones in warmer weather to be on the safe side.

You can also include herbal teas, use warm water to make your soups and nut milks with and warm up your food in a dehydrator before you eat them if you really miss the taste of a warm meal.

How long can you eat raw food for at a time?

You'll have to be the judge of that for yourself. I like to go raw for about 9 days at a time, but I have been raw for a 30 days. There are many people in the raw food world who have been fully raw for over a decade and several people have claimed they haven't eaten any cooked food for over 40 years. Just 3 examples are Storm Talifero (40yrs raw), Lou Corona (39yrs raw) and Annette Larkin (27yrs raw).

Can raw foods reverse degenerative diseases like cancer, heart disease and diabetes?

Your food is your fuel and your fuel is what allows every part of your body to function. If you aren't getting sufficient fuel, or the fuel you are getting is full of harmful additives, then it's only a matter of time before your body stops working properly, which includes being able to heal, repair and defend itself against diseases.

Give your body clean wholesome fuel, clean it up with regular cleansing habits and you'll be surprised what it can heal itself from. Raw foods, whole foods and organic foods are a big part of it, but a good diet with a positive mental attitude, professional support in some cases, exercise, hydration, discipline and cleansing are a winning combination.

Is it safe for children to eat raw foods?

There were some very disturbing cases of families whose children were taken away from them for a number of months because they fed them a raw vegan diet and were accused of neglect and abuse by doing so.

However the children had no signs of malnutrition or stunted growth at all.

There are also cases of children who have tragically passed away from malnutrition due to their parents feeding them a raw vegan diet in a dangerous way.

The media love a sensational story, so it would be interesting to find out the reality behind these stories, but nevertheless, it does highlight that, as with everything, there's a safe and unsafe way to do things.

Here is my advice to you regarding feeding your children raw foods

1. NEVER solely feed a baby under 18mths raw vegan foods without professional help, if at all. If you can't breastfeed but don't want to feed your baby commercial formula milk, seek professional advice from a qualified nutritionist about alternatives. Babies need a very specific balance of nutrients to survive until they can eat solids, don't guess, get professional help. DO NOT DO THIS ALONE.

2. Once a baby can eat solids, introduce raw and cooked foods to them equally and see which ones they react best to. But always ensure the foods are high quality, organic and very well cleaned.

3. When your child gets older, continue to include as many raw foods as they want, and no matter what you're feeding them, monitor your child and check them over regularly to make sure they are developing well and not showing any signs of deficiencies.

4. If your child thrives on mainly raw foods, with good energy, strength, mental agility and good immunity, with no signs of deficiencies or ill health, there is no reason not to continue them with high levels of raw foods.

To date, there is no scientific evidence that a child who is brought up on a raw vegan diet is any more or less at risk of degenerative diseases, mental health problems, physical development issue or anything else. But there are more and more families who are choosing to let their children eat a predominately 100% raw vegan diet and having great results.

Just 3 examples of families eating high levels of raw food are:

Victoria, Sergei & Valya Boutenko (www.rawfamily.com)
After using a raw food diet and green smoothies to help transform her own health and overcome her son's juvenile diabetes, mother of 2, Victorie Boutenko began to thoroughly research the health benefits of green smoothies and raw foods and wrote the very popular book The Green Smoothie Revolution' and many more books since then. Her son Sergei and daughter Valya have both followed in her footsteps by writing books and recipes helping people improve their health naturally with raw foods and healthy living.

Storm & Jingee Talifero (www.thegardendiet.com)
This couple of raw vegan activists and educators, (Storm has been a raw vegan for over 30 years now) have 5 children (between 4 – 18years old) who have all been on a raw vegan diet for the majority of their lives. During a documentary they produced called 'Breakthrough' they took their children to get checked at the doctors and all 4 children who were around at the time the film was made, showed good levels of health and normal development for their ages.

Ka and Katie Sundance (www.therawfoodfamily.com)
This couple have 5 children, have been predominantly raw for nearly 9 years and have only just started to add grains a few times a week to their lives, They are very active on YouTube where you can follow their journey, but the interesting thing with them is that they get their full blood levels checked for most nutrients every year and they have never come up with any major deficiencies to date, even the mother who's been pregnant of breastfeeding almost constantly for the whole time (a bit like me).

I must confess…
Sadly, I used to use my own children as an excuse for not going 100% raw vegan when things weren't going well for me. I had convinced myself that they wouldn't like the foods I was making and that I didn't know enough recipes that they could survive on and it was too difficult to make different meals for all of us in that case.

Once I realised that I'd never actually **tired** to introduce more raw foods into their diet and started too, I realised that not only did they really enjoy most of the meals I made them (they are children so can be decidedly picky at times), even if they didn't really like them, they would always agree to finishing their meals (just about). Adding more raw foods definitely gave them more energy and even seemed to relieve some digestive symptoms they experienced.

They now eat some raw foods at least 2-3 times a day and I can still see the benefits.

Another thing to bear in mind is that the number of children who are suffering daily from malnutrition, abuse, deformities, chronic disease, mental and emotional problems, whilst eating a **cooked diet**, far outnumber the handful of cases that make it to the news of raw vegan or vegan children who end up with one of the above.

It's very easy for us to blame the part of a situation that seems most alien to us, as the cause when something goes wrong, instead of looking at the situation as a whole. For example, in one of the cases of a raw vegan child who passed away, even though the parents were initially accused of neglect, it was discovered that the child had a genetic defect that caused their illness and it was unlikely that any diet would have caused or prevented it, so they were cleared of all charges against them.

My spiritual guide and master teacher Dr Malachi K York taught me that the only constant is change, so if what you are currently feeding your children and yourself is producing ill health, you can't expect to keep eating it and get different results as that would be insane.

Make positive changes to your children's and your own diet by adding some of these delicious recipes and see the improvements, I'm sure you won't be disappointed. But remember, keep a good eye on them and note any changes, for the better or the worse, and respond accordingly.

Why do you have to soak the nuts, seeds and grains in these recipes?
Nuts, grains and seeds naturally have substances called enzyme inhibitors on them to protect them from rotting in nature until they find suitable conditions to grow into a new plant. These enzyme inhibitors can block the absorption of nutrients when we eat them and make the nuts, seeds and grains much more difficult for our bodies to digest and get the nutrients from.

The simple process of soaking nuts and grains for between 5-8hrs and seeds for 2-3hrs, helps release these enzyme inhibitors and makes them live, which means they are ready to start growing and sprouting, which also increases the level of nutrients and live enzymes in them. Once soaked, you can use them in wet recipes like a bread mixture or smoothies, or you can dry them in a dehydrator so you can use them in dry recipes again, like piecrusts or ground into flours or just for snacking.

Instead of soaking and drying small individual batches for each recipe, I tend to soak and dry lots at a time and store them either in the fridge or in an air tight container in a cool dry cupboard so they are ready as soon as I want to make something with them.

"Soak And Sprout Grains, Nuts And Seeds, To Give Your Body The Nutrients It Needs"

Leah Salmon

9 Tips To Raw Success

1. Hydrate & cleanse – The more water you drink and the more you gently cleanse your system, the more you will benefit from the higher level of nutrients in raw foods.

2. Transition at your own pace – Day by day, week by week, month by month, build up at a pace that is comfortable to you, this is not a race, it's a journey and being 100% raw full time isn't the finish line, it's still just part of that journey if you choose to go in that direction long term. So around your 9 fully raw days, just do what feels right to you.

3. Keep it varied – Get as much variety into your meals as possible, they'll be a lower chance of getting bored or missing out on any nutrients,

4. Get your mind ready for it – The increase in energy, mental clarity and emotional stability you get when you increase the raw foods in your life, can trigger some great things to happen. Prepare to go through some kind of transformation, no matter how big or small, don't be afraid of new feelings and perspectives arising, or a sense of needing to make big changes in other areas of your life. Remember, the only constant is change.

5. Supplement – The unfortunate reality is that the soil most of our food is grown in is devoid of many nutrients, which means the food that is grown from it is going to be lacking nutrients too, so finding natural supplements to boost your missing nutrients may be necessary, which can be herbs, sea vegetable & algae or even fruit and vegetable super foods.

6. Listen to your body – Feeling anything but good after eating anything, cooked or raw, is a possible sign that the food wasn't right for you. Respond to the signals your body gives you. If something constantly makes you feel bad leave it out, if something constantly makes you feel great, bring it on!!!

Also listen to your tummy!!! Portion control, calorie counting and weighing and measuring food is not a requirement at all. If you are still hungry after a meal, eat a bit more until you're full and make a bigger portion next time. If you're stuffed half way through a meal, stop eating, save it in the fridge until later and make a smaller portion the next time.

7. Be honest with yourself – If at any point it begins to feel wrong in anyway, be honest with yourself and move on in a way that feels most comfortable for you. There are 8 different meal plans to choose from at the back of the book, which you can use to guide your journey.

8. Hygiene – This is very important with raw foods, wash and store all your food carefully and eat organic and chemical free wherever possible.

9. Get support – This can be one to one private support, an online forum, a good book (like me!), a course, workshop or a group of friends who all decide to do it together. There really is strength in numbers and getting support from someone or others who have been where you are before is priceless. Check out the Useful Links page at the end of the book for more useful resources.

"A Generation On Whole Foods Will Turn Hospitals Into Museums"

Leah Salmon

7 Signs That You Need To Get More Raw Food Into Your Diet, Quick!!!

- You burn almost everything you cook

- You still think that a salad won't fill you up, even though you've never tried one (a good one, not a plate of soggy Iceberg lettuce)

- The only green leaf you have, comes as the garnish on your entree at a restaurant

- The last time you had an apple it was in a pie from the freezer

- You can count on one hand the number of portions of raw fruit and vegetables you've had in the last 7 days

- When you see someone soaking nuts, seeds, grains or beans you get scared something will start growing from them (when that's actually the point!!!)

- You think raw pizza is made from uncooked pizza dough and cold tinned pizza sauce!

Sound anything like you?!? Well let's get some super raw goodness into you quick!!!

My Top 6 Equipment List

There are a few essentials you need to get started with raw foods, there are also some luxuries that can be added if you fancy. But beware of gadgets, I've bought one too many of these that end up being used once & never again, will I ever learn?

A good knife and chopping board - There will be some days when this is all you need to prepare all your meals. Having a good sharp knife to tackle all those juicy fruits and vegetables can make things easier, just be careful with it.

A Jug Blender - Most of the drinks in this book and in most raw food recipes are made in a blender, so are many sauces, dressing and dips. The harder the ingredients, the more powerful your blender needs to be.

At the top end of the market you have the Vitamix and Blendtec blenders, which are very powerful and produce exceptionally smooth products very quickly and cost between £450-600 each. At the lower end of the scale you can find a high street brand of blender or a Nutribullet blender for between £30 - £150. The cheaper blender can still create some pretty fantastic results, so get what you can, but obviously aim for the best.

A Food Processor - This is used more for processing dryer ingredients like bread and Burger mixtures, some sauces and dips too. You can also grind down nuts and seed quite well with them (but not flaxseed). These range from £30 - £250, so again decide what works best for you.

Dehydrator - If you like burgers, pancakes, crackers, breads and very well marinated foods, then definitely invest in one. They work by blowing hot air over the foods to remove the moisture (i.e dehydrating them), which intensifies the flavour, and you set it to a temperature of no higher than 40°C to retain the most nutrients. They range from £30 - £300 and are widely available. 15 of the recipes in this book need one, but there's the 'Juicy Plan' of dehydrator free recipes if you really don't want to use one. Find out more about them on the next page.

Nut Milk Bag – I make nut milk a lot and the smoothest milk is produced when you strain it with a nut bag, so it's a handy thing to have around and very affordable at around £2. You can even use it to strain juices made in a blender or with more bits than you like. You can make your own bag with a piece of cheesecloth, but not regular strainers as their holes are too big. Some people will even use a new pair of tight for this job, but I've never tried that!

Grinder – Ground flaxseed are in most bread, pizza base, pancake and wrap recipes, which you'll need a grinder to make. High speed blenders, nut mills or the grinder attachment you get with some food processors and blenders are the only things that can grind flaxseed and store bought ground flaxseed doesn't compare in price or nutrition. It can also make flours from nuts, seeds & grains so they are very useful.

A Word On Dehydrators

Some people see these as a fad in the raw food diet that process food in an unnatural way, by removing a vitally important nutrient, water. For this reason some people choose not to use them, It's definitely best not to over do dehydrated food, especially if you already don't drink enough water, but used responsibly, I feel dehydrated food has a place in the raw vegan diet. I use mine about 2 -3 times a week while on raw, as I really love foods like raw breads, avocado fries, corn chips, and kale chips, but mine broke and I didn't replace it for over 8mths and we did just fine enjoying all the other delicious raw foods nature had to offer.

A Healthy Option - If you or your family are currently eating processed, junk foods like potato chips, wheat bread, foods fried in cheap oil or anything with trans or hydrogenated fats, MSG or aspartame, trust me, replacing them with some dehydrated foods you've made from scratch is a MASSIVE improvement and can help to wean you off those foods for good, while adding more natural foods to your diet.

Safety - When dehydrating foods, it's important to ensure they are fully dried if you're going to store them for any length of time, otherwise they'll rot while in storage and become unsafe to eat. If you're drying foods for a long period of time, ensure your dehydrator is set to over 35 degrees so it dries at a stead pace. If after 10-12hrs of drying something, it's still very moist, it may begin to go off as it wasn't dried on a warm enough setting. Following the instructions in the recipes and storing foods properly will keep you perfectly safe.

What can you dehydrate? Most fresh fruit and vegetables that are fit to eat can be dehydrated, so you can add them to dishes or preserve them for long periods of time. Drying guides can be found online to dry anything from garlic chips, to lemon peels to dried tomatoes. NEVER dehydrate food that has spoilt or is starting to spoil.

Cost of Running A Dehydrator - Even though they are on for hours at a time, they actually take very little electricity to run and manufacturers pride themselves on producing machines that use as little electricity as possible and even brag about it in their literature.

Find them online by searching for 'food dehydrators'

29

Top Ingredients List

There are a few common ingredients that appear in a lot of recipes that you may want to stock up on (as well as loads of fresh greens, vegetables and fruits!!!)

Garlic – This seems to work well with many dishes as a natural seasoning and I personally love the flavour.

Limes and lemon – The juice gives foods a certain lift, similar to adding salt or vinegar and a good preservative, especially of colour.

Virgin Coconut Oil – This oil is exceptionally good for you and acts as a thickener, creamer and enriches many foods.

Extra Virgin Olive Oil – This lovely rich oil goes well with dark green leafy vegetables and again thickens and enriches sauces.

Maple Syrup & Honey– Maple syrup is not RAW (shock horror!!!) but you can get raw honey. These are the most natural liquid sweeteners that work great with raw recipes.

Dates – These sweet sticky things bind pie crusts and sweets together with nuts perfectly. They are a very natural sweetener, but can contain glucose syrup and sulphur dioxide, so read the label. There are a few different types of dates (Champagne, honey, medjool etc) some softer and sweeter than others, so just use the one you prefer.

Celtic or Himalayan Salt – Regular table salt can have an array of other chemical ingredients in them and virtually no nutrition. Good quality sea salt, Celtic, grey, black and pink Himalayan salts normally have no other ingredients, but naturally contain a good level of nutrients, especially minerals.

Almonds - A mild tasting popular nut that works well in many recipes.

Macadamia nuts or cashews – When soaked and blended, there are few other raw vegan foods that can achieve the same smooth, silky, creamy 'dairy-like' consistency they do.

Bananas – These thicken shakes and add a soft sweetness to many desserts.

Romaine Lettuce – I had almost completely lost faith in lettuce until I heard about romaine lettuce. It's big strong leaves make it a handy plate for main meal dishes and it has a refreshing light taste as you would expect from a good salad leaf.

Avocados – If you do better on fats and proteins, keep a good stock of these to add a clean source of fat to main meals and even some breakfasts and desserts.

Tomatoes – They are sweet and juicy and a perfect addition to any salad. Sun dried tomatoes have a richer flavour making them great to blend into sauces.

Flaxseed - You'll want to stock up on this if you intend on enjoying dehydrated breads, crackers and pancakes. Ground flaxseed is second to none in raw food recipes for holding things together. I use the brown more that the golden.

"If At First You Don't Like Greens
Juice Them & Try Again"
Leah Salmon

Drinks, Juices & Smoothies

Given the chance, I would happily live on 3 smoothies a day, a vegetable salad and a fruit salad for my whole 9 days a month, but it doesn't always work out that way. Most drinks will last in the fridge for about 24hrs, so you can store any remaining portions for later.

Drinks, smoothies and juices made from wholesome whole foods is such a good way to get masses of nutrients into your body in one go, but bear in mind, it can be difficult to eat 10 oranges in one go, without feeling stuffed afterwards and not needing more food, so make a juice with as many oranges as you could eat in a sitting, so your body can handle the high level of nutrients that's coming in.
(inspired by Dr Malachi Z York's book – Purity & Neatness)

Be creative, have fun and stay juicy!!!

PEPPERED STEAK

Slow-cooked tender British beef in black pepper sauce with peas & carrots.

CHICKEN & MUSHROOM

Roast chicken & chestnut mushroom in English Mustard sauce.

LAMB SHANK

3-hr slow roasted & hand-pulled British lamb shank with peas & carrots.

VEGGIE DELIGHT

Butternut squash, chestnut mushroom, leeks & spinach in cream sauce.

VEGAN

Butternut squash, chestnut mushroom, leeks & spinach in coconut milk.

For Best Results:

1. Decant from freezer to fridge to defrost overnight. (NEVER attempt to defrost at room temperature or in microwave).
2. Preheat your oven INCL. BAKING TRAY to 220°C / 200°C fan / Gas M. 7, for 15 mins.
3. Remove outer plastic covering (do NOT remove foil pie tin), and rest at room temperature until top softens slightly – about 5 mins.
4. Brush top of pies with beaten egg or milk wash.
5. Place pies on hot baking tray and place in middle of oven. Set timer for 15 mins
6. After 15 mins, reduce heat to 200°C / 180°C fan, Gas M 6. Reset timer for 15 mins.
7. After 30 mins total baking time, remove and allow pies to cool ON hot tray for 5-10 mins before eating. If top appears sunken in the middle, replace in the oven for a further 5-10mins

Easiest Method (Cook from Frozen):

1. Preheat your oven INCL. BAKING TRAY to 200°C / 180°C fan, Gas M 6, for 15 mins.
2. Remove outer plastic covering (do NOT remove foil pie tin), and rest at room temperature until top softens slightly – about 5 mins.
3. Brush top of pies with beaten egg or milk wash.
4. Place pies on hot baking tray and place in middle of oven for 35-40 mins.
5. Remove and allow pies to cool ON hot tray for 5-10 mins before eating. If top appears sunken in the middle, replace in the oven for a further 5-10mins

Ovens vary so treat the above as guidelines only.
Products are not suitable for microwave cooking.

Best Before: See bottom of pie tin

PEPPERED STEAK

CHICKEN & MUSHROOM

Green Power Juice

A definite favorite in our house, especially in the evening before bath time for some reason. Serves 2-3.

You'll Need:
1 big handful of kale
1 cucumber (with the skin)
4 celery sticks
1 lime, peeled
4 apples (Braeburn, Pink lady and Jazz are our favorites, but the choice is yours)

You'll need to: Wash the kale, celery, cucumber and apple, then juice them in your juicer with the lime and enjoy.

Pear, Apple & Ginger Juice

In my humble opinion, nothing goes better with pear in a juice than hot ginger and sweet apples. Serves 2.

You'll Need:
3 apples
3 pears
1 inch of fresh ginger root peeled

You'll need to: Put the apples, pears and ginger through a juicer, then add the water afterwards

Apple, Carrot & Celery Juice

I used to make this with broccoli instead of celery and it didn't make that much juice, I now much prefer the celery version for the taste and the quantity produced. Serves 3.

You'll Need:
4 apples cored and quartered
A head of celery or 8 stalks washed topped and tailed
6 carrots, washed, topped and tailed
1 lime, peeled
1 cup of water

You'll need to: Wash and prepare all the produce, then put the apples, carrots, lime and celery through a juicer, then dilute with the water afterwards.

Leah's Tips: Protein types can cut out the lime and add some spinach to this juice. You don't have to dilute it, but it can help if you have blood sugar imbalances.

Apple Ginger Lime Drink

A quick, mild yet refreshing juice, made in a blender and strained. Serves 3.

You'll Need:
1 lime peeled
1/2 inch slice of ginger root, peeled
3 apples cored and quartered
4 cups of water

You'll need to: Put everything into a blender and blend until everything is broken down then strain. You can store this in a glass bottle in the fridge for about 2 days, shake well before drinking.

Red Power Juice

Fresh raw beetroot can sometimes be a little harder to find than the cooked version, but you'll need the raw ones for this juice. Beetroot is very cleansing to the blood and digestive system, whilst being a great energy booster. Serves 2.

You'll Need:
1 raw beetroot bulb
2 carrots topped and tailed
2 apples cored and quartered
3 celery sticks
½ cucumber
½ cup of water

You'll need to: Wash and prepare all the produce, then put the beetroot, apples, carrots, cucumber and celery through a juicer, then dilute with the water afterwards.

Green Smoothies

There is an entire revolution going on in the name of these wonderful drinks, started in part by Victoria Butenko following Dr Ann Wigmore's energy soups and live food programs and continued by many other raw food experts to date.

I have found them to be the perfect way to get raw dark green leafy vegetables into children's diets and a very filling nutritious meal or snack.

There are so many varieties of green smoothies, which are essentially just a combination of fruits, vegetable and green leaves, but here are just a few you can try:

- **Mango & Spinach** – Blend the flesh of 1 large mango with 1 handful of spinach with a little water until smooth

- **Orange, Banana & Spinach** – Blend 2 peeled and seeded navel oranges (the medium sized ones) or 2 cups of orange juice with 2 bananas, 2 handfuls of spinach and ½ cup of water until smooth

- **Apple, Pear & Romaine** – Blend 1 apple cored and chopped, 1 pear chopped and cored and 4 large well washed romaine lettuce leaves very well until smooth

- **Spinach & Sprouts** – Blend 1 handful of spinach, ½ cup of alfalfa sprouts, 2 romaine lettuce leaves, 2 ripe bananas and ½ lime until very smooth

- **Kale, Cucumber & Celery** – Blend 2 big kale leaves or 2 handfuls of chopped kale (storks removed either way), 2 celery stalks, 1/2 whole cucumber, 1 lime, 1 banana and 1 cup of apple juice (or 2 apples) until smooth.

- **Strawberry, Banana, Mango & Romaine** – Blend 10 strawberries (leaves removed), 2 bananas, the flesh of 1 mango and 4 romaine lettuce leaves with ½ cup of water until smooth

- **Pineapple, Strawberry & Spinach** – Blend ½ a medium pineapple peeled, 1 cup of strawberries with the stalks removed and 1 handful of spinach with 1 cup of water until smooth.

Leah's Tips: Adding a squeeze of lemon or lime juice to smoothies (if they don't already have lemon or lime in them) can help smoothies last in the fridge for 24hrs and you can make they a bit more energizing and filling by adding 1tbsp of coconut oil to them.

Peach Berry Smoothie

A nice simple combination that also freezes well into lollies for a summer snack. Serves 2.

You'll Need:
6 ripe peaches
1 banana
1 cup of strawberries or raspberries
½ cups of water

You'll need to: Destoned the peaches, peel the banana and wash the berries, then add everything to a blender and blend until smooth.

Leah's Tips: Protein types can add hemp protein powder, sprouts or coconut oil to this smoothie if needed.

Pina Colada

Once you've cracked the coconut, the rest is as easy as pie. Serves 2-3.

You'll Need:
1 lime peeled
2 bananas
½ a pineapple peeled and chopped
1 brown coconut
3 cups of water

You'll need to: Make coconut milk by breaking the coconut open, cutting out the meat, then blending it with 3 cups of water and then straining the milk from the mixture. Pour the coconut milk back into the blender, add the bananas, pineapple and lime and blend until smooth. If you really don't want to crack open a coconut, you can make the milk from blending 1 cup of desiccated coconut in 3 cups of water and straining it, but I'd highly recommend making it fresh at least once for this recipe. The coconut pulp left over can be dried and used as coconut flour in many gluten free recipes.

Pink Carrot Smoothie

I don't normally make a drink with more than one machine, just to save on washing up to be honest! But this recipe only works well with carrot juice and is definitely worth the extra washing.

You'll Need:
3 carrot juiced
1 mango, peeled and cored
1 orange peeled and deseeded
2 bananas
1 cup of raspberries, fresh or frozen
1 cup water

You'll need to: Juice the carrots in a juicer, then pour the juice into a blender with all the other ingredients and blend until smooth.

Berry Yoghurt Smoothie

This is easily one of my favorite smoothies, which tastes just like a dairy yoghurt. Serves 2-3.

You'll Need:
2 cups of fresh or frozen berries (strawberries, raspberries, blackberries and blueberries works well) – preferably fresh
2 bananas
2 oranges peeled and seeded
2 tbsp of coconut oil
1 cup of water

You'll need to: Add everything to a blender and blend until smoothie and creamy.

Almond Milk (Basic Nut or Seed Milk)

This is the base of many milks and smoothies, but great alone too. Serves 2.

You'll Need:
1 cup of any raw nuts or seeds (almonds, brazil nut, sesame seeds, pistachio etc) soaked for 2-5hrs Or 3 tbsp of any nut or seed butter
3 cups of water

You'll need to: Start by pouring off the water the nuts/seeds have been soaked in and rinse them. Then blend them with 3 cups of water and press through a nut milk bag or fine strainer to produce your milk. You can either discard the pulp made, compost it or find another raw vegan recipe that can use it, there are quite a few around. If you're using nut or seed butter, then simply add it to 3 cups of water in a blender and blend until completely combined, that's it!!!

Chocolate Milk Shake

This recipe comes from the wonderful Carolyn Akens of www.carolynakens.com. Serves 2.

You'll Need:
2 cups of almond milk (made using recipe above)
1 frozen banana
2tbsp chocolate powder
2tbsp of maple syrup or honey
1tsp vanilla extract
1/8 tsp Himalayan pink salt
1/8 tsp cinnamon

You'll need to: Put all ingredients in a blender and blend on full power until smooth and creamy,

Tahini Carob Milk

I drank this every day when I discovered it some years ago and still use it often today, though sometimes replace the carob with chocolate powder and add kelp powder to enrich the drink even more. Serves 2.

You'll Need:
2 tbps of carob powder
3 big soft dates or 2tbsp of honey
3 tbsp of tahini
2 ripe bananas
3 cups of water

You'll need to: Put all the ingredients in a blender and blend until smooth

Hazelnut Hot Chocolate

There's a brand of commercial instant hot chocolate that uses hazelnuts and taste ok, but this is a much cleaner richer version, perfect to curl up with after a long day. Serves 2.

You'll Need:
1tbsp of hazelnut butter or ½ cup of hazelnuts soaked for 5hrs
1tbsp of raw chocolate (Cacao) powder
3 soaked dates or 2tbsp of honey
2 cups of very warm, but not boiling water

You'll need to: Make the hazelnut milk by straining and rinsing the soaked nuts, blending them in the water until they're completely broken down then straining the milk out. Now pour the milk back into the blender with all the other ingredients and blend until smooth. If you're using the nut butter, just add to the blender with everything else and blend.

Leah's Tips: Add vanilla extract or cinnamon for an even richer taste and replace the chocolate powder with carob if chocolate gives you any bad reactions.

Cocobana Milk

Another coconut based smoothie, this time with peanut butter or tahini. Serves 2

You'll Need:
3 cups of fresh coconut milk
1 banana
3 tbsp of peanut butter (no added sugar) or tahini
5 soft dates or 3tbsp of honey

You'll need to: Make the coconut milk using the basic nut or seed milk recipe on page 36, then put the milk and other ingredients into a blender and blend until smooth

Fuzzy Pink Lemonade

Another quick drink made in the blender then strained. Serves 3-4.

You'll Need:
2 limes peeled
1/2 inch chunk of ginger root, peeled
3 apples cored and quartered
2 cups of raspberries, fresh or frozen
3 tbsp of maple syrup, honey or 3 big soft dates
4 cups of water
2 mint leaves

You'll need to: Put everything into a blender and blend until everything is broken down then strain. You can keep this in the fridge for at least 2 days, shake before serving.

Kefir
(with Apple, Orange & Pineapple Soda version)

This fizzy fermented probiotic drink is a great alternative to sodas and fizzy drinks, which is a great nutrient booster. You'll need to buy water kefir grains or a water kefir starter kit, which is easy to find online and very affordable. Once you've made the first batch of kefir, you can save a small amount of it in the fridge and that's what you'll use to start the next batch of kefir, so a pack of kefir starter can last you months. Drink about 100-150mls a day.

Naturally boosting and maintaining the levels of friendly bacteria in your digestive system keeps your bowel movements regular, keeps your colon from becoming impacted with waste and improves the absorption of nutrients from your foods. Kefir also contains nutrients like vitamin B12, created during the fermentation process, which can be lacking in many people's diets. Don't worry about the sugar included in this recipe, the kefir starter grains or kit will use up all the sugar in the fermentation process so there'll be none left in the resulting kefir you'll be drinking.

NOTE – Read the instructions on the Kefir starter kit or water kefir grains packet as some are prepared differently than stated below. Once you've made your first batch you can use the methods below for the next batches

You'll Need:
A kefir starter packet or a tablespoon of kefir start grains
1litre of room temperature spring or filtered water (not tap water)
2 heaped tablespoons of organic cane sugar (you may not need this depending on the kit you buy)
The juice of a lemon
A clean large glass jar & lid (One big jar or smaller ones that can hold 1litre together)
A large plastic jug for mixing
A plastic, wooden or silicon spoon, not metal

You'll need to: Pour the room temperature water into the plastic jug. Add the kefir grains or sachet of the starter kit and stir. Then stir in the sugar and lemon until they are dissolved and pour into the glass jar or jars and cover with the lid. The lid can be placed on the top instead of tightly screwed on as pressure can sometimes build up inside the bottle.

Leave the bottle at room temperature for 24-48hrs until it's producing bubbles when you gently shake the bottle. Once it's fizzy, move it to the fridge where it will last about 2 weeks, any left after this time may not taste as good but keep it to start the next batch.

Want a different taste?
To make a fizzy juice drink with your favorite juice, simply add 50-100mls of a previous batch of kefir to 750mls – 1litre of freshly made pineapple juice, apple juice, orange juice or any other juice, place in a glass bottle and leave for 24-48hrs until fermented.

Your Recipe Notes

"A Generation On Whole Foods Will Turn Hospitals Into Museums"

Leah Salmon

Breakfasts

Many say breakfast is the most important meal of the day, no matter what time you eat it.

Getting live foods into your system after your body's natural elimination period (between 4 – 10am) is a great way to start the day and gently fire up your digestive system. Many of these breakfasts are fruit based, which can make some people hungry quickly.

If you find yourself hungry soon after these breakfasts, try adding a juice or smoothie to your meal or using a main meal as your breakfast instead, leaving these as snacks or desserts.

Remember to always listen to your body and not the clock to tell you when you're really ready to eat and just drink water until then.

Enjoy

Mango Shots

This is a light kicking breakfast for someone on the run. This makes enough for one.

You'll Need:
1 large ripe mango
2 tbps of fresh lime juice
2 – 3 fresh mint leaves

You'll need to: Peel and dice the mango flesh, finely chop the mint and then mix together with the lime juice.

Melon Bowl

I love melon for breakfast, as it's a quick fresh water filled breakfast that tastes great, especially in the warmer months. Serves 1.

You'll Need:
½ Gala, honeydew or cantaloupe melon
A big wedge of watermelon

You'll need to: Scoop the seeds out of your melon half, and then slice out the flesh inside to make chunks. Cut the watermelon into chunks, mix the two melons together and refill the hollowed out melon halves.

Banana Split

Typically an ice cream filled desserts, but in my house it's a fruit filled breakfast fit for a king, a prince and some little princesses! Serves 4.

You'll Need:
4 medium bananas
1 soft ripe pear
2 cups (400g) strawberries
2 mangos
1 cup of Macadamia nut Cream (from page 52)

You'll need to: Peel a banana, lay it on its side and slice it in half lengthways. Pull the skin back and leaving the banana inside, slice it up and open it to form a gap down the middle

Now wash and chop the pears, strawberries and mango and fill each banana with an equal amount of the chopped fruit and serve with a dollop of macadamia cream.

Leah's Tips: This is a perfect meal to make with your children. You can add any variety of fruit to fill it and like the traditional one; you can add ice cream if you choose instead of macadamia cream (see Chocolate ice cream recipe page 99).

Banana Nut Pudding

This is thick, creamy pudding that you can quickly whip up for a satisfying breakfast. Serves 2.

You'll Need:
2 large ripe bananas
2 tbsp of nut butter (hazelnut, peanut, almond or brazil nut are good)
The jelly of 2 young green coconuts (aka Jelly or Thai coconuts) & ½ cup of its water
2 tbsp of chopped pecans
3 soft dates or 2tbsp of honey
A pinch of salt

You'll need to: Add everything except for the pecans to the blender and blend until smooth and lump free. Serve in a bowl topped with the chopped pecans or fresh fruit.

Mango Avocado Pudding

This thick, creamy and satisfying pudding can be watered down into a smoothie or even frozen into an ice cream or lolly. Serves 2.

You'll Need:
1 large ripe mango
1 medium avocado (the Hass variety of avocado works well)
The jelly of 1 young green coconut (aka Jelly or Thai coconuts)
3 soaked dates or 2tbsp of honey
2 tbsp of fresh frozen rock rose bee pollen (optional)
2tbsp of coconut water from the coconut (optional)

You'll need to: Simply add all the ingredients to a blender or food processor and blender until smooth. Serve as it is or topped with the fresh frozen rock rose bee pollen for a delicious and very nutritious finish. If it's too thick, add the coconut water and blend again.

Hi Enz Mix

Another thick filling porridge/pudding, which is also rich in live enzyme due to how it's prepared. Serves 2-3.

You'll Need:
3tbsp almonds
2tbsp brazil nuts
1tbsp of pumpkin seeds
2tbsp sunflower seeds
1tbsp of hazelnuts
½ cup of buckwheat
5 dates or 3tbsp of honey
2 tbsp raisins
1 banana
A pinch of salt
1 cup of coconut meat or desiccated coconut & 3 cups of water
1tbsp of cocoa powder and a pinch of cinnamon (optional)
400ml of coconut milk or water and 2tbsp of coconut oil
½ cup of fresh berries

You'll need to: Put the almonds, pumpkin seeds, sunflower seeds, hazelnuts, brazil nuts and buckwheat in a bowl and cover in filtered or spring water. Then put the raisins and dates in another bowl with 1 cup of filtered or spring water to soak. Leave them both soaking over night or for at least 5 hours.

Next make the coconut milk by blending the 1 cup of desiccated coconut or coconut meat with the 3 cups of water until fully broken down, then strain the milk out and keep half the pulp to add to the recipe.

When you're ready to make it (as a filling meal anytime of the day), drain and rinse the bowl of nuts and seeds, then put them in a blender, pour the other bowl into the blender with the water it soaked in and add the banana, salt, cocoa powder and 2 cups of the coconut milk and it's pulp.

Blend everything until all the ingredients are completely broken down and a thick creamy pudding is formed. Top with fresh berries, cinnamon or a topping of your choice and enjoy.

Leah's Tips – You can actually use any combination of nuts and seeds to make this pudding, so if you prefer to use macadamia nuts, cashews, sesames seeds, chia seeds or flaxseeds that's fine, the point of the meal is to create a filling creamy breakfast pudding to replace oats, which is easy to digest from the soaking, enzyme rich and of course YUMMY!!!

These ingredients are enough for about 2-3 bowls or 1 big bowl, but you can pre mix the nuts and seeds to save time measuring them out at each meal and then use 9tbsp of the mixture added to the buckwheat, dates, coconut etc.

Spiced Buckwheat Porridge

A simpler version of the Hi-Enz mix with fewer ingredients and a unique and delicious taste. Ideal for cold winter mornings. Serves 2.

You'll Need:
½ cup of buckwheat soaked in water for 5hrs of overnight
5 dates or 3tbsp of honey or maple syrup
1 banana
A pinch of salt
½ tsp of mixed spice
1 cup of fresh coconut milk or 1 cup of water and 2tbsp of coconut oil
100ml of freshly boiled water

You'll need to: Drain and rinse the buckwheat, then put all the ingredients into the blender and blend until a smooth creamy porridge is created.

Vanilla Chia Pudding

To boost your Omega 3 fats for brain health and gorgeous skin and hair, add this recipe to your weekly meal plan. I don't use vanilla beans often due to convenience and cost, but they were worth it in this recipe. Serves 2.

You'll Need:
¼ cup of chia seeds
1 ½ cups of fresh almond or coconut milk
1 vanilla pod
3tbsp of honey or maple syrup

You'll need to: First make your coconut or almond milk (recipe from page 38). Then slice the vanilla pod open and scrap the seeds out. Now stir the chia seeds, honey/maple syrup and vanilla beans into the milk and let them all soak for 10-15mins and serve.

Leah's tip: You can pre soak the chia seeds (1/4 cup seeds to 1 ½ cups milk or water) and they can last in the fridge like this for about 3-4 days, so you can quickly add to smoothies and puddings. It is a bit more difficult to stir the honey and vanilla into the soaked chia seeds, which is why I combined them first then soaked them in this recipe.

Muesli

Inspired by Karen Knowler The Raw Food Coach, it took me a while to find the combination that worked best for me and here it is. Play with different ingredients until you find the mix for you. You can combine the dried fruit and nuts in an airtight container in large quantities and just prepare the fresh fruit when you come to eat it to save time. This has been a BIG hit at every raw food workshop I've hosted. Serves 3-4.

You'll Need:
¼ cup of chopped almonds
¼ cup of chopped Brazil nuts
2tbsp hazelnuts
¼ cup of dried coconut
2tbsp raisins
5 stoned dates chopped
A pinch of cinnamon
1 apple cored and diced
1 banana sliced
1tbsp of honey or maple syrup
¼ cup of fresh raspberries, blueberries or mango
2 cups of any nut or seed milk (recipe on page 38) (I normally use almond or coconut milk)

You'll need to: Once you've made the nut milk, simply mix the nuts, dates and raisins in a bowl and mix well, pour on the milk and top with the fresh fruit, honey or maple syrup and cinnamon then serve and enjoy!!!

Strawberry Pancakes & Cream

When I discovered the raw vegan pancake recipe and realized how quick and easy it was, tears of joy almost came to my eyes!!! I love crepes and pancakes, many vegan gluten free cooked ones just don't taste right to me at all, but these bad boys are a winner. You can enjoy 2 big or 3 smaller pancakes from this mixture. Serves 2-3.

For the pancakes you'll need:
4 ripe bananas
1 cup of ground flaxseed
A pinch of cinnamon
A pinch of salt
For the macadamia cream you'll need:
4 big soft dates
1 ½ cup of macadamia nuts soaked for 5hrs or overnight
1 cup water
You'll also need:
2 cup of strawberries chopped

You'll need to: Put the bananas, salt, cinnamon and flaxseed in a food processor and process until a lump free batter is produced. Pour the batter into big round pancakes on a teflex or other dehydrator sheets and dehydrate for 2hrs, then flip and dehydrate for another 2hrs until dry and pliable.

How to make the cream
Put the soaked macadamia nuts, water and dates into a blender and blend until a smooth cream is formed. You may need to use a tamper (if you have a Vitamix or other blender with a tamper) to push the mixture down to the blades and move it around. You may even need to stop the blender once in a while and push it down then start it again to keep it going.

To assemble, put ½ of the strawberries and cream in the center of each pancake, then roll or fold the pancakes up and tuck in, triple yum!!!

Leah's Tips: You can replace the flaxseed with Brazil nuts that have been soaked and ground for a slightly different taste, but you'd need to dehydrate it for a few hours longer.

If you make the pancakes and cream the night before, you can assemble this breakfast in a few minutes by just washing the strawberries and wrapping everything up. You can make the pancake mixture, dry it for 2 hours, then flip it and let it dry through the night so it's ready and warm in the morning.

Granola Berries & Cream

I saw a picture of this in a magazine and decide to create a raw vegan version to have as a special breakfast and voila!!! Here is it!!! Serves 3.

You'll need:
1 cup of almonds
½ cup of dried coconut
½ cup of sunflower seeds
¾ cup of dried dates
A pinch of salt
2 cups of frozen or fresh raspberries
2 cups of chopped mango

For the cream you'll need:
4 big soft dates or 3tbsp of honey
1 ½ cup of macadamia nuts soaked for 5hrs or overnight
1 cup water

You'll need to: First make the granola by adding the almonds, coconut, sunflower seeds, dates and salt into a food processor and process into crumbs.

How to make the cream
Put the soaked macadamia nuts, water and dates into a blender and blend until a smooth cream is formed. You may need to use a tamper (if you have a Vitamix or other blender with a tamper) to push the mixture down to the blades and move it around. You may even need to stop the blender once in a while and push it down then start it again to keep it going. If it's really stuck, drizzle in more water as it blends until it gets going.

Now to assemble this lovely treat! Get a glass, put a layer of raspberries, then some mango, then some granola, and then some cream and top with more raspberries and mango. You can make it more exciting with more layers (i.e. berries, cream, granola, mango, cream, granola, cream, berries, mango then granola).

Leah's Tips: You can add any variety of fruits to this dish; other combinations that work well are bananas and strawberries or pineapple and kiwi. The contrasting colors of the fruits make this a visually tasty morning treat too.

Your Recipe Notes

Snacks, Dips & Sides

It's always a good idea to have wholesome snacks around to compete with all the junk food snacks that we're surrounded by daily.

Whether it's an addition to a main meal, an afterschool snack before dinner or something to take with you on your travels; these are going to be very helpful.

Enjoy

"Commit to whole foods and herbs to create the health you deserve"

Leah Salmon

Red Pepper Dip

The sweetness and flavor of the red pepper and the creaminess of the nuts are what make this dip so special. Enjoy this with crudités (sticks of vegetables), crackers, as a salad dressing, the mayo on coleslaw or with any cooked foods you.

You'll Need:
1 cup macadamia soaked for 4hrs
¾ cup water
2 tbsp of lime juice
2 cloves of garlic
¼ tsp salt
2 soft dates or 1 tbsp of honey
1 sweet red pepper (capsicum) seeded and roughly chopped

You'll need to: Add everything to a blender and blend until smooth, stop the blender and mix the mixture to help the process and add very small amounts of additional water if needed. If you have a high-speed blend with a tamper, use this to move the mixture round.

Vinaigrette

A classic salad dressing world over, which lasts weeks in a sealed bottle in a cool dry cupboard or the fridge.

You'll Need:
1 cup of extra virgin olive oil
4 tbsp of tamari
1/3 cup of apple cider vinegar or ¼ cup of balsamic vinegar
¼ cup honey or maple syrup

You'll need to: Mix all ingredients together in a bowl with a wire whisk or fork or put into a jar with a lid and shake well until combined.

Orange & Mango Dressing

A tangy juicy dressing for a light salad, courtesy of from Carolyn Akens
www.carolynakens.com

You'll Need:
½ cup of orange juice
The flesh of ½ a mango
3tbsp of olive oil
¼ tsp salt
3tbsp of lime juice
1tbsp of maple syrup or honey
1tsp of tahini
1/8 tsp cayenne pepper

You'll need to: Put everything into a blender and blend until smooth.

Pear & Mint Dressing

Inspired by a Russell James' recipe, this creamy and unique tasting dressing is for those with a more adventurous palate.

You'll need:
2 ripe conference pear
1 avocado
½ cup of macadamia nuts soaked for 5hrs
½ cup of pure water
¼ cup of fresh mint leaves
3 dates soaked for 30mins

You'll need to: Wash, core and chop the pear, peel and remove the stone from the avocado, then add everything to a blender and blend until very smooth.

Almond Mayo

This versatile sauce is my first choice when I need something creamy to jazz up a salad, pasta or pizza base.

You'll need:
1 cup of almonds soaked for 5hrs
¼ cup of lemon juice (the juice of about 1 whole lemon)
1 clove of garlic
¼ tsp of salt
¾ cup pure water

You'll need to: Put all the ingredients into a blender and blend until smooth. Store it in an airtight container in the fridge and it will last 3 days.

(Right Chickpea humus – Left Almond Mayo)

Chickpea Humus

It you like cooked humus, you'll love this one ☺ & it lasts in the fridge for days.

You'll Need:
1 cup of chickpeas soaked for 8 hrs then drained & left at room temperature for 8hrs
3 cloves of garlic
¼ cup of olive oil
¼ cup tahini
1tsp turmeric
1 tsp cumin
¼ of lemon juice (the juice of about 1 whole lemon)
½ tsp salt and ¼ tsp cayenne (optional)

You'll need to: Put everything into a food processor and process until smooth. You may need to stop the machine to scrap it down from the sides if it's sticking.

Cheese Sauce

Nutritional yeast & turmeric give this recipe a taste and colour reminiscent of cheese.

You'll Need:
1 cup macadamia nuts soaked for 5hrs
1 cup water
4tbsp olive oil
3 heaped tbsp nutritional yeast
½ tsp turmeric
½ tsp salt

You'll need to: Put everything in a blender, blend until smooth and enjoy.

Hot Sauce

Inspired by Debrose Searchwell from LibRaw, this will give a spicy kick to your meals.

You'll Need:
1-2 red scotch bonnet peppers deseeded and chopped (its best to wear gloves)
¼ cup of honey or maple syrup
¼ cup of apple cider vinegar
¼ cup of olive oil
2 cloves of garlic
6-6 sundried tomatoes soaked for 10mins in hot water or the ones, which come in oil
1tsp of salt

You'll need to: Simply put everything in a blender and process until smooth.

Spicy Avocado Dip

A super quick dip to prepare, with a citrus and spicy kick.

You'll Need:
2 ripe avocados
3tbsp of lime juice
¼ tsp cayenne
A pinch of salt
2 baby plum tomatoes chopped to garnish

You'll need to: Simple mash the avocados, stir in the lime juice and salt, then top with the cayenne and tomatoes, Ready in 5mins flat and great on crackers or lettuce.

Curry Sauce

Another quick yummy sauce or salad dressing that lasts 3-4 days in the fridge.

You'll Need:
½ cup of olive oil
¼ cup of orange juice
1 apple
The juice from half a lime
1tbsp of curry powder
½tsp of salt

You'll need to: Put all the ingredients into a food processor and process until smooth and creamy.

Kimchi

Naturally fermented foods are a great source of friendly bacteria, vitamins and minerals and very easy to make at home yourself, just like the Kefir recipe on page 41. Enjoy this sour tart addition to any meal.

You'll Need:
½ head of white cabbage grated
2 carrots peeled and grated
2 cloves of garlic crushed
2 inch of ginger root diced
1tbsp salt

You'll need to: Place all the ingredients in a large bowl, mixing the salt into the vegetables very well. Then with a meat mallet or something heavy with a flat bottom, pound the vegetables continually for about 5 minutes until you can see water being released from them.

Transfer the mixture to a large glass mason jar with a lid and press down the vegetables until the liquid comes over the top of them, then loosely cover the jar and store in a dark cupboard for about 3-5 days to ferment, then finally store the jar in the fridge where it will last for months.

Sunflower Pate

A thick, spreadable, filling pate, which goes perfectly with crackers and salads

You'll Need:
1 cup of sunflower seeds soaked for 2hrs then rinsed and drained
1 carrot peeled chopped
¼ white onion
2tbsp of chopped fresh coriander
½tsp of salt & ¼ cup of olive oil

You'll need to: Put all the ingredients into a food processor and process until smooth.

These 2 recipes will last in the fridge for 5 days, can be frozen for 3mths and if completely dry, can be kept in a cupboard in an airtight container for a few weeks. Use them as a pizza base, bread for a sandwich or burger or to accompany a soup. These ingredients will make about 4-5 cups, which is 3-4 batches

Courgette (Zucchini) Bread

Courgettes have a mild taste and are a very cost effective way to bulk up raw bread or cracker recipes, which you can add many flavors to.

You'll Need:
1 large courgette chopped
1 medium onion chopped
1 cup of ground flaxseed soaked in 1 cup of water for 2hrs
½ cup of buckwheat soaked for 5hrs
½ tsp of salt & ¼ cup of olive oil

You'll need to: Process all the ingredients in a food processor apart from the flaxseed, then when all the other ingredients are broken down, add the flaxseed and process until everything is combined. Spread about 1-1 ½ cups of the mixture on to a dehydrator sheet or baking paper greased with olive oil, in any shape you like, just make sure it's even and not too thick (about ¼ inch deep). Dehydrate for about 4hrs until dry on top. Then flip it over onto the tray, carefully peel off the sheet scraping off any batter stuck to it and spreading it back on the base and dehydrate for another 4hrs or until dry throughout.

Tomato & Buckwheat Bread

Another raw bread recipe with a slightly sweeter tomato taste.

You'll need:
1 cup of buckwheat soaked for 5hrs
1 cup of ground flaxseed soaked in 1 cup of water for 2hrs
3 medium tomatoes chopped
1 medium onion chopped
¼ cup of olive oil and ½ tsp of sea salt
¼ cup of fresh coriander
¼ cup of fresh flat leaf parsley
¼ cup of sundried tomatoes soaked for 30mins in warm water or the oil packed ones

You'll need to: Put the buckwheat, tomatoes, onion, salt, olive oil, sundried tomatoes, parsley and coriander into a food processor and process until broken down, then add the flaxseed and process until combined. Spread about 1-1 ½ cups of the mixture on to a dehydrator sheet or baking paper greased with olive oil, in any shape you like, just make sure it's even and not too thick (about ¼ inch deep). Dehydrate for about 4hrs until dry on top. Then flip it over onto the tray, carefully peel off the sheet scraping off any batter stuck to it and spreading it back on the base and dehydrate for another 4hrs or until dry throughout.

Flax crackers

A favorite in the raw food world, which lasts weeks in a cool dry cupboard or frozen.

You'll Need:
1 cup of ground flaxseed soaked for 2hrs in 1 cup of water
1 large onion chopped
2 cloves of garlic
2 carrots grated
½ tsp salt
¼ cup of olive oil
½ cup fresh coriander

You'll need to: Process all the ingredients in a food processor apart from the flaxseed, then when all the other ingredients are broken down, add the flax and process until everything is combined. Spread about 1-1 ½ cups of the mixture on to a dehydrator sheet or baking paper greased with olive oil, in any shape you like, just make sure it's even and not too thick (about ¼ inch deep). Dehydrate for about 4hrs until dry on top. Then flip it over onto the tray, carefully peel off the sheet scraping off any batter stuck to it and spreading it back on the base and dehydrate for another 4hrs or until dry throughout.

Kale Chips

I absolutely love these chips, you can use the long black kale leaves (cavolo nero) or the bag of chopped leaves, either way, they're a big hit of nutritious deliciousness! .

You'll Need:
1 cup macadamia or cashew nuts soaked for 5hrs then drained
½ cup water
2tbsp olive oil & ½ tsp salt
1 sweet red pepper deseeded
6 – 8 whole kale leaves or 3 cups of chopped kale
2 cloves of garlic
3 tbsp of lemon or lime juice (about half a lemon or lime)
¼ tsp of cayenne (optional)

You'll need to: Put the nuts, water, pepper, salt, lemon juice, olive oil, garlic and cayenne (if you're using it) into a blender and process into a smooth sauce. Then wash the kale, cut each big leaf into 2 – 3 pieces if using the whole leaves, then coat the kale in the sauce (all the pieces if using the chopped kale or both sides of the big leaves) and dehydrate them for about 8 hours until completely dry, flipping them over half way.

Avocado Fries

These taste like fries so much it's amazing and they're a huge hit with all my children too.

You'll Need:
3 ripe avocados
½ cup of ground flaxseed
½ tsp of cumin
½ tsp of salt
¼ tsp cayenne
¼ tsp of granulated garlic (optional)

You'll need to: Make the coating by mixing the flaxseed, cumin, salt, cayenne and garlic well in a bowl. Then peel and half the avocados, remove their seeds and slice them lengthways into strips, but not too thinly. Coat each strip In the coating, place them on a dehydrator sheet then dehydrated for 3hrs on one side, then flip and dry the other side for 3hrs or until slightly crisp.

Corn Chips

Fancy a tortilla chip? Well here you have it!!!

You'll Need:
3 cobs of sweetcorn with kernels sliced off (about 2 cups of kernels)
½ a white onion
1 peeled and grated carrot
½ tsp of salt
1 clove or garlic chopped
¼ cup of olive oil
½ cup of ground flaxseed soaked in 1 cup of water for 2hrs

You'll need to: Process all the ingredients in a food processor apart from the flaxseed, then when all the other ingredients are broken down, add the flax and process until everything is combined. Spread about 1-1 ½ cups of the mixture on to a dehydrator sheet or baking paper greased with olive oil, in a square and make sure it's even and not too thick (about ¼ inch deep). Dehydrate for about 4hrs until dry on top. Then flip it over onto the tray, carefully peel off the sheet scraping off any batter stuck to it and spreading it back on the base and dehydrate for another 4hrs until dry throughout. Once dry, cut into triangles with a sharp knife and enjoy.

Fried Mushroom

A tasty topping to salads, burgers, pizzas or soups, you can dry these for less time for a softer result or longer for a dryer slightly crunchy treat.

You'll need
1 cup of sliced organic mushrooms
¼ cup of olive oil
2 cloves of garlic crushed
¼ cup lemon juice

You'll need to: Combine the olive oil, lemon juice and garlic to make a marinade, then wash and slice the mushrooms and pour the marinade over them and stir them together well, making sure all the mushrooms are coated with the marinade.

Let the mushrooms marinade for about 30mins then spread them over a dehydrator sheet and dehydrate for 4-6hrs.

Your Recipe Notes

_____

_____

_____

_____

_____

_____

_____

_____

_____

_____

_____

_____

_____

_____

_____

_____

O L P F U Z E R R C I U I
I O D I M T E U M X N W F S W S R V K I L F
J M V Z L G P J B Y B M J C N Z M Z H A G D
N E O Z E K C Q V O H Q U J G A W C W S A Q
L E O C P K T X J X D T O N T E B D W G I I
B K E V O I K V O S G R K W J F C M U F Y
J C Q U G X Z J J Y N X A C Q W G R D F I
F X X R N K F U M X F Z Z T C V O D R S
R H L O S T E T I B B R G T S Z V Y L
C E P E I N K X C O L L J R B H Y S O K
Y Y H B P D Q Y J I A U D H V C W J M I
A G L G J E A O M I O Y P O R X D O W
Z G X E B L E F O U N D S H S I B T
E A F F P H M B G B Y Y P C N H I O
I O U L L W S H D E T R
V U B W I

"Maintaining your health is easier than regaining your health"

Leah Salmon

Main Meals

Lunches and dinners are traditionally the bigger meals in day and for those who think raw vegans are stuck with simple salads for all our meals, think again!

You can enjoy burgers, pizzas, spaghetti, rice dishes, tuna salad, coleslaw, wraps and soups to rival any cooked alternative.

Enjoy!!!

Creamy Green Soup

I've enjoyed every green soup I've tried so far and I realize that's mainly because they all have this same deliciously simple base, which on its own is quite enough. Serves 3.

You'll Need:
3 avocados
1 cucumber
¼ cup of lime juice
1 large or 2 smaller cloves of garlic
¼ cup of coriander (cilantro)
3 big soft dates or 2tbsp of honey
2tbsp of extra virgin olive oil
½ tsp of salt
1 ½ cups of pure water
3 romaine lettuce leaves
½ chopped tomato to garnish

You'll need to: Put all the ingredients, except the tomatoes, into a blender and blend until smooth and lump free. Pour into bowls, top with chopped tomato & enjoy! If it comes out to chunky, you can juice the cucumber first then blend it's juice with the other ingredients.

Leah's Tips: You can also top with sweet corn, chopped red bell pepper, parsley, mint leaves or even a swirl of almond mayo

Butternut & Tomato Soup

If you like creamy tomato soup or you miss tinned cream of tomato soup, check out this yummy soup recipe. Serves 3.

You'll Need:
2 cups butternut squash peeled & diced (about 1 small or half large squash)
2 cloves of garlic
2 fresh basil leaves
¼ cup of extra virgin olive oil
4 medium fresh tomatoes
½ tsp of salt
1 ½ cups of very warm pure water
3 big soft dates or 2tbsp of honey
¼ cup of sundried tomatos soaked or the ones packed in oil

You'll need to: Put all the ingredients in the blender jug to soak, making sure that the dates and sundried tomatoes in particular are in the water for 30mins, then blend until smooth and enjoy.

Cream of Courgette Soup

The miso (if you choose to use it) and dill give this soup a rich and distinctive taste and it's quite filling too. Serves 2-3.

You'll need:
1 cup water, plus additional water to thin
2 medium courgettes, peeled and chopped
2 stalks celery, chopped
2 tbsp lime juice
2 tbsp olive oil
2 tsp white miso (optional)
2 small cloves garlic, crushed
1/2 teaspoon Himalayan Pink salt, or to taste
1/8 tsp cayenne
1 avocado, mashed
2 tbsp minced fresh dill (or 2 teaspoons dried)

You'll need to: Place the water, courgettes, celery, lime juice, olive oil, miso, garlic, salt and cayenne in a blender and process until smooth. Add the avocado and dill and blend briefly. Add additional water to thin the soup if if's too thick, and blend. Serve chilled or at room temperature. It can be stored in a sealed container in the refrigerator for up to three days.

Mushroom Soup

Wild or shitake mushroom taste great in this recipe but choose your favourite organic variety. Serves 2-3.

You'll Need:
½ cup of almond soaked for 5hrs
1 ½ cups of warm water
2 cups of your favorite organic well washed mushrooms
2 cloves of garlic
2 big soft dates or 1 tbsp of honey or maple syrup
½ tsp of salt
¼ cup of olive oil

You'll need to: Make warm almond milk by blending the soaked almonds in the water fully then strain the milk from the pulp. Blend the milk with the well washed and chopped mushrooms, dates/honey/maple, garlic, salt and olive oil until smooth and creamy. Enjoy.

Coconut Curry Soup

A rich creamy coconut based soup, made from mature brown coconut milk, with a spicy kick and a gorgeous yellow colour. Serves 2-3.

You'll Need:
The meat from 1 brown mature hairy coconut & 3 cups of warm water
1tsp of curry powder (mild, medium or hot depending on how hot you want it)
1 tbsp of lime juice
2 medium tomatoes
2 cloves of garlic
2 big soft dates or 1tbsp of honey
½ tsp of salt
¼ cup of olive oil
1 inch chunk of root ginger peeled
3-4 sprigs of flat leaf Parsley or coriander leaves torn into pieces

You'll need to: Crack open the brown coconut with hammer (be careful not to hurt yourself) and break the meat out. You can use some of the coconut's water in place of some of the warm water in the recipe.

Now make coconut milk by blending the meat with the water and straining the resulting milk out. Now put the coconut milk in a blender with the curry powder, lime juice, 1 ½ tomatoes, garlic, dates/honey/maple, olive oil and ginger and blend until very smooth.

Pour the finished soup into bowls, dice the remaining half of a tomato and stir in, along with the parsley or coriander leaves and enjoy.

Eggless Egg Salad

This recipe is inspired by Matt Amsden book Rawvolution, which was a blissful discovery for me. His book is a definite favorite of mine and I highly recommend it. The turmeric is what gives the boiled egg taste in the recipe and the brilliant colour. Serves 3.

You'll Need:
1 ½ cups macadamia soaked for 5hrs and drained
1 clove of garlic
The juice of 1 lemon
1 tsp of tumeric
½ tsp of salt
1 cup of water
3 handfuls of any salad leaves (very well washed bagged salads work well)
½ red bell pepper, deseeded and sliced or diced

You'll need to: Put macadamia nuts, garlic, turmeric, lemon juice, water and salt into a blender and blend until smooth. Wash the salad leaves, make a bed of them on a plate and pour the egg salad on top, then garnish with the red pepper and enjoy.

Kale, Mango & Tomato Salad

I'm such a big fan of kale, even though I only discovered it a few years ago, and combined with my 2 other favorite foods makes this a treat for me. It's a visually appeal dish which is filling and very nutritious. Serves 3.

You'll Need:
4-5 cups of chopped washed kale
12 cherry or baby plum tomatoes
4 tbsp of extra virgin olive oil
1 ripe mango diced
½ tsp of salt
½ tsp cumin

You'll need to: In a large bowl, massage the oil, salt and cumin into the kale leaves until they are dark green and glistening. Then top with the mango and tomatoes and enjoy.

Tuna Salad

I found out that if you want something to taste like fish, dill and lemon do this well. This is what you find in hollandaise sauce, which frequently tops fish meals, and it's what makes this yummy salad so reminiscent of tuna. Serves 4.

You'll Need:
1 cup of soaked and drained macadamia nuts
2 cups of soaked sunflower seeds
¼ cup of fresh dill chopped
2 cloves of garlic
½ cup of lemon juice (about 2 lemons)
½ tsp of salt
2 tsp of mustard powder
¼ cup of olive oil
¾ cup of pure water
4 sticks of celery diced

You'll need to: Make the dressing by blending the macadamia nuts, garlic, salt, lemon juice, mustard, olive oil and water until smooth. Put the sunflower seeds in a food processor and process into crumbs. Then mix them with the celery and dill and pour on the dressing. Mix everything thoroughly and enjoy.

Pretty Salad

I've been trying to convince my children that courgettes aren't the worst thing in the world, but in salads like this one, the courgette bread and the spaghetti, they don't even notice it's there, result!!! Serves 4.

You'll Need
1 courgette washed and grated
1 cucumber washed and grated
2 carrots washed, peeled and grated
1 cup of radishes washed and grated
2tbsp maple syrup or honey
2tbsp olive oil
1tbsp apple cider vinegar
A pinch of salt

You'll need to: Simply mix the courgettes, cucumbers, radishes and carrots in a bowl, then in another bowl make the dressing by combining the olive oil, vinegar, maple syrup or honey and salt. Pour the dressing over the salad, mix well and enjoy.

Wild Bloomed Rice

This recipe is a good reminder of the taste of cooked food while you go raw for a little while. You can combine it with any vegetables, but I found these work well. Please don't try this recipe with white or brown rice only raw wild rice. Serves 3-4.

You'll Need
½ cup of wild rice
2 tomatoes chopped
3 tbsp olive oil
¼ tsp salt or 2 tbsp of tamari
¼ cup of chopped parsley
¼ tsp chilli flakes (optional)

You'll need to: Start by blooming the rice. Wash it a few times then soak it in a large glass bowl in 2 – 3 cups of fresh water for 3 days, changing the water twice a day. After 3 days, rinse and drain it fully, pat it dry with a paper towel so it's not too wet, add the tomatoes, salt or tamari, olive oil, parsley and chilli flakes, stir well, serve and enjoy.

Super Sprout Salad

Sprouts are an absolute powerhouse and anything that contains them deserves the title of SUPER!!! Including this delicious salad. Serves 3-4.

You'll need:
3 cups alfalfa sprouts or 3 tbsp of Alfalfa seeds to sprout (directions below)
2 grated carrots
1 cup of baby leaf spinach finely sliced
1 avocado sliced
3 tbsp of sesame, flax or hemp oil
1 pinch of sea salt
(Optional\) 3 tbsp of seaweed flakes or chopped seaweed paper or sheets

You'll need to: Start by sprouting your seeds if you're using seeds. To do this, soak the seeds in a large glass jar, covered with a piece of muslin, the lid of the jar with holes poked into it or some kind of mesh to allow air to circulate. Let them soak overnight or for at least 5hrs. Then rinse in fresh water and drain fully.

Now leave the seeds in the empty jar with it's covering for 3 -4 days until they fully sprout and each seed has a 1-2cm sprout growing from it. Rinse and drain the seeds and sprout twice a daily while growing and then put them in the fridge once fully grown. If they begin to rot at any point during the process, throw them out but as long as you rinse them with fresh water daily & drain them fully this is unlikely to happen.

Now simply combine 3 cups of the sprouts with the carrots, spinach, seaweed (if using) and avocado, drizzle on the oil, sprinkle with the salt and enjoy.

Fruit & Veg Salad

Add a little more sweet juiciness to your meal with this fruit filled salad. Serves 2.

You'll need:
1 apple cored and sliced
1 clementine or Satsuma peeled and separated
A small bunch of red grapes or about 15-20
2 romaine lettuce leaves
½ a cucumber thinly sliced
1 cup of lambs lettuce or baby leaf spinach

You'll need to: Combine all the ingredients together in a bowl and serve with a dressing of your choice. The Orange & Mango Dressing from page 59 goes great with this meal.

Tabouli

I got told off on YouTube for calling this recipe Tabouli as it doesn't contain bulgur wheat, but hey, I'm exercising my culinary creative license and to me it tastes very similar to the Tabouli I first had from my Iranian friends mother as a teenager, so sue me ☺. Serves 2-3.

You'll Need
1 cup of almonds soaked for 5hrs
1 cucumber diced
3 medium tomatoes, chopped
4 chopped spring onions (scallions or green onions)
½ cup fresh chopped parsley
1 clove garlic, minced
½ cup fresh chopped mint
¼ cup of lime juice (about 1 ½ limes)
3 tbsp of Extra virgin olive oil
½ tsp salt

You'll need to: Process the almonds in a food processor until they are finely ground then pour them into a large bowl with the cucumber, tomatoes, spring onions, parsley, mint and garlic and mix.

Then combine the olive oil, lime juice and salt before pouring it over the other ingredients and mixing very well. You can eat it straight away or let it marinate for 30mins before tucking in. Either way, enjoy.

Spicy Sweetcorn Coleslaw

Coleslaw is a true classic side dish and this raw version is a perfect alternative.
Serves 3-4.

For the Almond Mayo You'll Need:
1 cup of almonds soaked for 5hrs and drained
¼ cup of lemon juice (the juice of about 1 whole lemon)
1 clove of garlic
¼ tsp of salt
¾ cup pure water
For The Salad You'll Need:
2 carrots peeled & grated
¼ large or ½ a small white cabbage grated
¼ tsp cayenne
½ medium white onion diced or 2 spring onions chopped to add some green
The corn sliced off 1 sweetcorn cob.

You'll need to: Mix the grated carrot, cabbage, onion, cayenne and sweetcorn together in a large bowl. Then make almond mayo by blending the almonds, lemon juice, garlic, salt and water until smooth. Finally pour the almond mayo over the vegetables, mix very well so the mayo coats all the vegetables and enjoy.

Mango Salsa

I've never been convinced about mango being in a salad, but my super star sister chef made it for me and changed my mind completely. Thanks Che. Serves 2-3.

You'll Need
2 ripe mangos peeled and diced
3 large tomatoes chopped
½ cup of fresh coriander finely chopped
½ a small red onion diced
2 tbsp of olive oil
A pinch of salt
(Optional) ¼ chilli flakes
(Optional) 1 tbsp of lime juice

You'll need to: Simply Combine all the ingredients in a bowl, mix well and enjoy. Add the chilli flakes for a fiery kick and lime juice for some zestiness.

Easy Peasy Pizza

You can whip up this bad boy in 10 minutes flat and be as adventurous as you want with the toppings. Serves 4.

You'll Need:
2 cups of almonds
¼ cup extra virgin olive oil
A pinch of salt
2tbsp of pure water
4 large tomatoes sliced
The corn sliced off 1 sweetcorn cob
8 fresh basil leaves
1 cup of Cheese Sauce (page 61)

You'll need to: For base process the almond, olive oil, salt and water in a food processor to make a crumbly dough. Pour it onto a plate and shape it into a pizza base shape with your hands by pressing it down, slightly wet or oiled hands can help you shape it more easily. Then top with the cheese sauce, tomatoes, basil, sweetcorn and any other toppings you like.

It can be a bit crumbly when transferring to different plates, so you may need to use a cake slice to lift each slice. Alternatively you can split the mixture into 4 and make 4 mini pizzas on each person's plate then top each one with ¼ of the toppings.

Fried Mushroom, Kale & Olive Pizza

Fried mushrooms are the perfect addition to this pizza, but you could use marinated or fresh ones if you 'd prefer. Serves 4.

For the pizza base, use either
1 Flax cracker (page 65)
Or 1 Courgette bread (page 64)
Or 1 Tomato & buckwheat bread (page 65)
For the cheese or pizza sauce, use either
½ cup of cheese sauce (page 61)
Or ½ cup of Almond mayo (page 60)
Or ½ cup of Tomato sauce (page 89)
For the toppings you'll need
½ cup of Fried mushrooms (page 67)
1 cup of chopped kale
1 cup of chopped tomatoes
1 tsp dried oregano
3 tbps of olive oil
¼ tsp of chilli flake (optional)
3 tbsp of chopped green or black pitted olives

You'll need to: Assemble the pizza on a dehydrator tray by spreading the cheese sauce, almond mayo or tomato sauce over the pizza base of your choice and putting all your toppings on top, with the olive oil being drizzled on last. Put the whole pizza back into the dehydrator for about 30mins until the kale has softened. Slice into pieces and enjoy.

Mushroom & Walnut Burgers

These burgers seem to go down well with burger and meat fans trying raw foods, as they are rich and filling. Great with a dollop of mayo, some fried mushrooms and a big salad. Makes about 10 burgers.

You'll Need:
1½ cups of walnuts soaked 2hrs, rinsed, then soaked for another 2hrs and drained
3 sundried tomatoes soaked for 30mins or oil packed ones
2 cups of sliced mushrooms
2 medium carrots grated
2 cloves of garlic crushed
¼ cup of fresh flat leaf parsley
¼ cup of fresh coriander
3tbsp of olive oil
½ tsp of salt

You'll need to: Put all the ingredients into a food processor and process until it resembles a burger mix. Then make burger shapes about 3" wide and 1 1/2" deep on a dehydrator sheet or baking paper and dehydrate for 3 hours, then flip and dehydrate for a further 2 hours. Serve immediately or store in the fridge for up to 2 days.

Veggie Burgers

A milder fresher tasting burger that isn't dehydrated, so it can be made quickly for a filling addition to your meal. Makes about 6 burgers.

You'll Need:
1 cup of chopped mushrooms
1 cup of chopped cauliflower
¼ white onion chopped
1 medium carrot grated
2 cloves of garlic crushed
¼ tsp of salt
1 tsp of lime juice
¼ cup of fresh flat leaf parsley
½ of olive oil

You'll need to: Put all the ingredients into a food processor and process until it resembles a burger mix. Then take a ½ cupful of the mixture and form into burger shapes with your hands onto a plate or you can put a metal cookie cutter on a plate, fill it with the mixture, press it down inside then carefully slide it off.

Falafel

I used to have to travel from Harlesden to Camden to get good falafel when I first became vegetarian, now you can get some pretty good ones in almost all supermarkets and you can whip up these raw ones in a few minutes too. Makes about 12 balls.

You'll Need:
1 cup of sunflower seeds soaked for 2hrs and drained
2 celery stalks
2 medium carrots grated
2 cloves of garlic
3 sundried tomatoes soaked for 30mins or oil packed ones
¼ cup of fresh coriander
3tbsp of olive oil
1tsp of ground cumin
½ tsp of turmeric
½ salt
½ cup of sesame seeds

You'll need to: Put all the ingredients apart from the sesame seeds into a food processor and process until everything is fully broken down and combined. Pour the sesame seeds into a shallow dish. Then form the mixture into balls about the size of a tennis balls with slightly wet hands.

Roll each ball into the sesame seeds to coat them lightly and then serve straight away or you can dehydrate them for 3hrs before serving. Either way, enjoy!!!

Greens, Beans & Rice

This is one of the densest most filling meals in the book and a new raw version of the worldwide favorite, beans and rice. Get ready to chew chew chew!!! Serves 4.

For the rice you'll need:
2 medium parsnips peeled
2tbsp of pine nuts
¼ cup of olive oil x 2
¼ tsp of salt
For the greens and beans you'll need
¼ cup of mung beans soaked for 12hrs, then drained and sprouted for 1-2 days, rinse 2-3 times a day
1 cup of parsley chopped
1 cup of cherry or baby plum tomatoes quartered
2-3tbsp of olive oil
A pinch of salt
2tbsp of lemon juice

You'll need to: Prepare the greens by mixing the sprouted mung beans, parsley, tomatoes, 2-3tbsp of olive oil, pinch of salt and lemon juice together thoroughly.

Next make the rice by adding the pine nuts, parsnips, ¼ cup of olive oil and ¼ tsp salt to a food processor and processing until they resemble small chunky pieces of rice. Serve the mung beans, parsley and tomato mixture on top of the parsnip rice with a few big romaine lettuce leaves and enjoy.

Plantain & Okra Stew

My parents are from Jamaica and Grenada, so they grew up on these 2 foods and I grew to love them as an adult, especially combined this way. Serves 2-3.

You'll need:
2 ripe plantains
12-15 okra (sometimes called lady fingers)
3 medium tomatoes
2tbsp of lime juice
3tbps of tamari
3tbsp of olive oil
¼ tsp cayenne (optional)
2-3 big romaine lettuce leaves

You'll need to: Simply peel and dice the plantain, top and tail the okra and dice, then dice the tomatoes and mix briefly together in a big bowl.

In another bowl, combine the tamari, lemon juice, cayenne (if using it) and olive oil and pour it over the plantain and okra and mix briefly again. Mixing the plantain too much can make it too mushy.

Let it marinate for about 15 – 20mins then serve on a large lettuce leaf each and enjoy.

Spaghetti & Sauces

I lived off spaghetti, pasta sauces, pesto and cheese in my vegetarian teenage years but they weren't as healthy as this. There are 2 sauces below, but any sauce you like is fine too. Want meatballs? Add balls of the Mushroom & Walnut Burgers on page 85. This recipe serves about 4 people, as you need about 1 courgette for 2 servings depending on their size.

For the pesto sauce you'll need
½ cup of fresh coriander
½ cup olive oil
½ cup of fresh basil
¼ cup of pine nuts
¼ tsp of sea salt
2 tbsp of green olives
1 clove of garlic
You'll need for the spaghetti
2 straight courgettes (zucchini)

For the tomato sauce you'll need
½ cup sundried tomatoes soaked for 30mins or the oil packed ones
3 dates soaked for 30mins
3 fresh medium tomatoes
¼ cup olive oil
¼ tsp of sea salt
½ tsp of dried oregano herb

You'll need to: Make the pesto by processing all it's ingredients until fully combined in a food processor. Make the tomato sauce by processing all it's ingredients until fully combined in a food processor.

Make the spaghetti by peeling the courgettes with a julienne peeler, which will slice it into strips (see bottom left), or a wide potato peeler, which creates wide flat strips, which you then slice into thin strips, or you can use a spiralizer or Spiroli machine to create them. Pour 1 cup of whichever sauce you're using onto the spaghetti, stir well to cover all the spaghetti and leave to marinade for between 5 - 30mins before enjoying.

Julienne Peeler and courgette spaghetti

Tomato sauce

Spaghetti & Tomato sauce meal

Humus & Cabbage Wrap

The sound of this recipe maybe unusual, but do give it a try and see how well these tastes complement each other. Serves 2.

You'll need:
½ cup of Chickpea humus from page 60
4 chopped tomatoes
½ a cucumber grated
1 grated carrot
2 whole lettuce leaves chopped
2 whole white cabbage leaves

You'll Need to: Mix the chopped lettuce, tomatoes, cucumbers and carrots together thoroughly. Wash the cabbage leaves, lay it out as flat as possible, spoon half the mixture into the middle of the leaf, then fold the sides to the middle, fold the bottom up a bit so the filling doesn't come out. They aren't the easiest things to wrap, so just do your best and enjoy.

Broccoli & Tomatoes with Tahini Dressing

Another gift from raw food chef & educator Carolyn Aken, which makes broccoli taste better than ever. Serves 2.

You'll need:
1/4 cup tahini
2 oranges, juiced
1 tbsp lemon juice
2 small or 1 medium head of broccoli
½ cup cherry tomatoes, halved
1 tbsp sliced almonds
¼ tsp Himalayan pink salt (optional)

You'll need to: First make the tahini dressing by blending the tahini, orange juice and lemon juice in a blender or with a hand whisk or hand blender. Shred the broccoli in a food processor or chop into small chunks then pour it into a bowl with the halved tomatoes and pour the tahini dressing and mix well. Plate the dressed broccoli and tomatoes and sprinkle the almonds on top.

Nori Sushi Rolls

Our children love eating the seaweed sheets so much I'm surprised I got a chance to make these!!! Enjoy this mineral rich dish with a big green salad and a smile.

You'll need:
1 Nori seaweed sushi sheet
½ avocado peeled, stoned, halved and sliced
5 baby plum tomatoes halved
¼ cucumber grated
¼ cup of alfalfa sprouts
2tbsp of Fried Mushrooms (page 62) or sliced pitted black olives
A pinch of sea salt or Himalayan salt

You'll Need to: Lay the Nori seaweed sheet down flat then start layering the ingredients down the sheet, just before the middle of it (see picture below), so there's enough sheet to fold over the filling to start rolling it. I normally put the avocado first, then the sprouts, cucumber, tomato then the olives or mushrooms. Sprinkle with the salt then fold the shorter side of the sheet over the filling and roll it to the end of the sheet to make a big roll. You can cut it in half or pick the whole thing up and eat it, either way, enjoy!

Leah's Tip: You can add Almond Mayo (page 60) to enhance the flavor but be sure not to let juicy wet fillings sit on the Nori sheet too long as it can get soggy and tear.

1. Lay it out

2. Add the filling

3. Roll it up

4. Slice in half and enjoy!

Spring Rolls

The rice paper you use to make these isn't raw, so you can choose to use a big soft lettuce leaf instead if you prefer. Serves 2.

You'll need:
6 spring roll wrappers or 4 soft round lettuce leaves
1 carrot grated
2 avocados diced
¼ cup coriander chopped
1 cup of spinach chopped
1 tomato
1 red bell pepper sliced
2 tbsp of Olive oil
2 tbsp of Tamari or a pinch of salt

You'll Need to: Prepare your filing by tossing the carrot, avocado, coriander, spinach, red bell pepper, tomato, olive oil and tamari/salt together briefly in a bowl. Now prepare the spring roll paper by placing one in a shallow dish of hot water for 10 seconds until it's soft, and then lay it out onto a flat surface.

Put 2-3 spoons of the filling in the middle of the sheet, fold the bottom up over the filling, then fold the sides over the middle, the roll it all up (see pictures below). Repeat with all sheets or leaves, serve and enjoy!

1. Add the filling **2. Fold the bottom up** **3. Fold one side over** **4. Fold the other side over**

5. Roll it up and enjoy!!!

Courgette & Avocado Rolls

You can use add as many different filing to these rolls as you like but the avocado taste really good with the courgettes. Serves 2.

You'll need:
1 straight medium courgette very thinly sliced (see picture below)
2 avocado
2 spring onions chopped
1 medium tomato diced
4tbsp of olive oil
A pinch of salt
2tbsp of lime juice

You'll Need to: Make the filling by mashing the avocados and mixing the spring onions, lime juice, tomatoes, olive oil and salt into it. Then place a heaped tablespoon of the filling onto the end of a strip of courgette, roll it up and lay it on a plate. You can use a little olive oil on the end of the courgette strip to make it stick to the roll or you can push the rolls onto bamboo kebab skewers or tooth picks if you want them to stand up.

Walnut Burritos

Walnuts give quite a meaty taste to a meal and make a great base for this simple and delicious recipe. This is very filling and will serve at least 4.

You'll need:
1 cup of walnuts - soak for 2hrs then rinsed and drain and repeat for another 2hrs.
1 cup of sunflower seeds soaked for 2hrs then rinsed and drained
½ red onion diced
3 tomatoes diced
¼ cup of fresh coriander chopped
2tbsp of olive oil
½ tsp of cumin
½ tsp oregano
½ tsp of dried garlic granules or garlic powder
¼ tsp salt
1 tbsp of honey or maple syrup
A pinch of chilli flakes (optional)
4 big romaine or other lettuce leaves

You'll Need to: Start by placing the walnuts, sunflower seeds, olive oil, cumin, oregano, garlic, salt, honey/maple syrup and chilli flakes in a food processor and pulse or process briefly to break down and combine the ingredients into a crumbly mixture.

Transfer the mixture into a bowl, add the tomatoes, onion and coriander and stir together. Then lay the lettuce leaf, pile a few spoons of the filling onto it, wrap the leaf around it and enjoy.

Your Recipe Notes

_____

_____

_____

_____

_____

_____

_____

_____

_____

_____

_____

_____

_____

_____

_____

_____

_____

Desserts

I love cakes, cookies, chocolate bars and fruits in general so this and the breakfasts are my favorite parts of the book.

There's a dessert for every taste, so I hope you find the one (or two!!!) for you.

Enjoy

Strawberry Lollies

My sister in law produced these one day when we went to visit, they went down a treat with the whole family. You can even get stainless steel or BPA free lolly molds to avoid the plastic ones. Makes about 6 lollies depending on the size of the mould.

You'll need:
3 cups of fresh strawberries
1tbp of honey or maple syrup
3tbsp of water

You'll need to: Once you've washed and removed the stalks from the strawberries, put about 5 aside, then add the rest to a blender with the honey/maple and water and blend until smooth. Chop up the remaining strawberries, stir into the mixture and then pour into ice lolly molds and freeze for 5-6hrs or until frozen solid. Run under a warm tap and wiggle them to pull them out of the mold and enjoy.

Rainbow Lollies

These take a bit of time to create, but the finished result is worth it, as they look great. Makes about 6 lollies depending on the size of the mould.

You'll need:
1 cup of fresh strawberries washed with stalks removed
1 cup of fresh blueberries washed
3 kiwis peeled
The flesh from 2 medium ripe mangos
1 cup of orange juice

You'll need to: First make the smoothies for the four layers by blending each different fruit with ¼ cup of orange juice until smooth. Then fill each mold ¼ full with the strawberry smoothie and freeze for 2hrs until the top of it is hard. Then fill it until it's half filled with kiwi smoothie, and return to the freezer for 2hrs until the top of that layer is hard. If the lolly stick or handle is long, stick it into this layer, if its short stick it into the next layer. Next fill it until it's ¾ full with the mango smoothie and freeze for another 2hrs and finally fill it to the brim with the blueberry smoothie and freeze for 3hrs to ensure everything is fully frozen. Run under a warm tap and wiggle them to pull them out of the mold and enjoy.

Mango Sorbet

You've probably guessed I love mango and this sorbet is so popular in the Salmon house that it's normally requested as a birthday breakfast with pancakes. Serves 4.

You'll need:
400g pack of frozen mango pieces or the flesh of 3 fresh mangos chopped and frozen for 5hrs or until hard
2 bananas peeled, chopped and frozen for 4-5hrs

You'll need to: Put the frozen mango and banana into a high speed blender and blend until smooth and creamy. If you have a less powerful blender, break it down in a food processor first then transfer to a blender to get it smooth.

Pink Ice Cream

To quote a customer who tried this recipe recently "It's amazing how the 3 main ingredients can transform into an ice cream that tastes so good!!!" Serves 3.

You'll need:
2 cups frozen raspberries or fresh raspberries frozen for 3hrs or until solid
2 oranges juiced or ¾ cup of fresh orange juice
3 bananas peeled, broken into chunks and frozen for 4-5hrs
(Optional) 1tbsp of fresh frozen bee pollen (I recommend the Rock Rose variety)

You'll need to: Simply put all the ingredients into a food processor or blender and process until smooth and ice creamy!!! If you find it too soft, put it back in the freezer for an hour or two to harden up. Top with fresh frozen bee pollen for added nutrients and taste.

Chocolate Ice Cream

There really isn't much that you miss out on when you eat more raw vegan foods, you even get to enjoy rich, creamy, decadent chocolate ice cream, aren't we lucky!!!
Serves 4-5

You'll need:
2 cups of macadamia nuts, cashew nuts or almonds (almonds not as creamy) soaked for 5hrs, rinsed and drained
¾ cup of dates soaked for 30mins
¼ cup of honey or maple syrup
2 ½ cups of water
2 heaped tablespoons of raw chocolate powder
A pinch of salt
(Optional) 1 large ripe banana

You'll need to: Simply blend all the ingredients until very smooth, and then freeze in a freezable container for 3-4 hours or until it's frozen throughout. If you have an ice cream maker, put the mixture in that and follow the instructions. Take it out of the freezer 10mins before you want to serve it and enjoy.

Tracker Bars

Though they aren't golden like the commercial tracker bars we get over here in England, these fruit and nuts bars really remind me of them. Makes about 6 bars.

You'll need:
1 cup almonds
1 cup of sunflower seeds
1 cup of desiccated coconut
1 cup of dates and ½ cup of raisins
A pinch of salt
2tbsp of coconut oil
½ tsp of cinnamon
¼ cup of ground almonds

You'll need to: Add everything, except the ground almonds, into a food processor and process until the mixture clumps together. Press it into a greased baking dish, chill for 1hr in the fridge, slice into bars then dust with the ground almond, or shape into balls and dust with ground almonds. Either way, enjoy!!!

Choco Snowballs

This recipe is inspired by a recipe for tiger nuts sweets in the book " Ancient Egypt and the Pharaohs" By Dr Malachi Z K York, my beloved teacher and spiritual guide, but with a few additions. Makes about 18-20 balls.

You'll need:
2 cups of almond
¼ cup of desiccated coconut
½ cup of dates
¼ cup of chocolate powder
2 tbsp of virgin coconut oil
A pinch of salt
½ cup of ground almonds

You'll need to: Put all the ingredients apart from the ground almonds into a food processor and process until it's all combined and it holds together when pressed. Shape it into about 18-20 balls. Put the ground almonds in a shallow dish or plate and roll the balls in it to fully coat them and you're done!

You can either chill them for 1hr or eat them straightaway. Either way, enjoy!

Fruit & Nut Bar

If you like the combination of raisins, nuts and chocolate like the popular English chocolate bar, then this recipe is right up your street. Makes about 4 bars.

You'll need:
½ cup of chocolate powder
¼ cup of coconut oil
¼ cup of maple syrup or honey
2tbsps of raisins
2tbsps of hazelnuts
A pinch of salt

You'll need to: Mix the chocolate powder, coconut oil, maple syrup/honey and salt together in a bowl until completely combined and thick chocolate sauce is made, then stir in the raisins and hazelnuts so they are evenly distributed throughout the mixture. Then spread the mixture into a small square or rectangular dish or form into a square shape on a plate and refrigerate for 1hr or freeze for 30mins until solid. Slice into bars and keep in the fridge or freeze until you're ready to eat them and enjoy!

Halva

This raw vegan version of a Middle Eastern treat takes just a few minutes to make and tastes rich and creamy. It's very dense so a little goes a long way. Serves 6.

You'll need:
1 cup of tahini
1 cup of ground almonds
¾ cup of honey or maple syrup
A pinch of salt
½ cup of sliced almonds

You'll need to: Simply put all the ingredients except the sliced almonds, into a bowl and mix with a strong big spoon until fully combined. Press the mixture into a small square or rectangular dish or form into a square shape on a plate and cover with the sliced almonds. Then refrigerate for 1hr or freeze for 30mins until solid and keep it in the fridge until ready to eat. Enjoy

Walnut Fudge

These become moister and buttery the more you process them, a really indulgent treat. You can prepare larger quantities of the walnuts and keep them stored so they're already soaked and dried and ready to use in this recipe or others. Serves 4

You'll need:
2 cups of walnuts soaked for 2hrs, rinsed and drained, soaked for 2hrs again, rinsed and drained again, then dehydrated for 5-8hrs
½ cup of date soaked for 30mins and drained
2 tbsp of virgin coconut oil
¼ cup of chocolate powder
1 ½ cups of desiccated coconut
½ tsp of vanilla extract & a pinch of salt

You'll need to: Add everything to a food processor and process continually until soft and buttery. Spread out into a shallow dish, refrigerate for 2 hours slice into squares and enjoy. Keep in the fridge until ready to eat.

Macaroons

Make loads of these yummy treats and store them in the freezer to snack on all day. Makes about 20 balls, which are best kept in the fridge until you're ready to eat them.

You'll need:
3 cups of desiccated coconut
¼ cup of coconut oil
¼ cup of maple syrup/honey
½ tsp of vanilla extract or the beans scraped from 1 vanilla pod & a pinch of salt

You'll need to: Process 2 cups of the coconut in a food processor until it's a soft almost buttery consistency, which can take about 5 minutes. Stop the machine to push the coconut back down to the blades if needed, and then add all the remaining ingredients and process again fully. Shape into balls, freeze for 1-2hrs & enjoy.

Carob Fudge Cake

This treat takes minutes to make with just a spoon and bowl and serves 4.

You'll need to:
2 cup of desiccated coconut
4tbsp of honey or maple syrup
2tbsp of carob powder
3tbsp of water & A pinch of salt

You'll need to: Mix all the ingredients together in a bowl thoroughly, spoon it out onto a plate, shape it into a cake shape and sprinkle some more coconut over it.

Carrot Cake & Lemon Frosting

A worthy opponent of the cooked version, this cake and its frosting are deliciously carroty, lemony, moist and delicious. Serves 6-8.

For the cake you'll need:

3 cups of grated carrot
1 cup walnuts soaked for 4hrs and rinsed
¾ cup date soaked in 1 cup of water – keep ¼ cup of the soaking water
¼ cup raisins, soaked for 30mins
1 1/2 tsp mixed spice
¼ tsp sea salt
2tbsp lemon juice

For the frosting you'll need:

2 cups of cashew or macadamia nuts
¼ cup of lemon juice
¼ cup of maple or honey
1 tsp vanilla extract or the beans from 1 vanilla pod (optional)
1/4 cup of coconut oil
¼ of water

To make the cake you'll need to: Put the carrots, walnuts, dates. date water, salt and spice into a food processor and process until smooth. Transfer the mixture to a bowl and stir in the raisins the press into a cake tin, pie pan or just shape it into a cake shape on a plate with wet hands. .

To make the frosting, you'll need to: To make the frosting put the macadamia or cashew nuts, lemon juice, maple syrup/honey, vanilla (if you're using it) and coconut oil into a food processor and process until smooth and creamy. Spread a thick layer of the frosting onto the cake and round the sides if you want, slice and enjoy.

Melon Party Cake

I've seen pictures of fancy cakes like this online and I've always wanted to make one, so when it was 3 of our children's joint birthday party, here's what I created. Serves 10-12.

You'll need:
1 small watermelon peeled
2 Galia or cantaloupe melons
1 cup of red grapes
1 cup of green grapes
2 cups of strawberries
3 medium oranges (navel oranges are good) peeled and sliced
3 kiwis peeled and sliced
Wooden kebab skewers you can break

You'll need to: Use the picture below as a guide to putting this cake together. Start by slicing the watermelon in half and place the halves on a display tray so they make two domes. I then broke the kebab skewers in half and threaded the grapes on in alternating colours and stuck them into the melon domes. Now make basket from the smaller melons by cutting a wedge from either side of the top of the melon, but leaving a 1" thick piece at the top to use as the handle (see the picture below). Then scoop out the inside of the melon with a spoon and slice a little of the bottom off so it can easily stand on the tray and fill them with most of the strawberries, leaving about 10 aside. Finally arrange the orange and kiwi slices on the tray to fill the empty space and scatter the remaining strawberries. You can easily stick candles into it for a birthday cake and hand out bowls for your guests to help themselves, enjoy!!!

Tropical Cheesecake

Even though the recipe looks intense, it's a really easy recipe to make. It's also very attractive on display and tastes wonderful. You don't need to top it with tropical fruit either, strawberries, raspberries, mango & banana or blueberries all work well too. Serves 8-10.

For the crust you'll need:
2 cups of almonds
1 cup of desiccated coconut
1 cup of dates
A pinch of salt
2tbsp of coconut oil

For the topping you'll need:
The flesh of 1 large mango sliced
1 cup of strawberries sliced
2 kiwis washed peeled and sliced
1 ripe passion fruit

For the filling you'll need:
2 cups macadamia or cashew nuts soaked for 5hrs
½ cup maple syrup
¼ cup of lime juice
½ cup of melted coconut butter/oil
A pinch of salt
1 tsp vanilla extract or the seeds from 1 vanilla pod
1 cup of dried coconut or mature coconut meat
3 cups of water

You'll need to: First make the pie crust by putting all the crust ingredients in a food processor and processing until it becomes a crumbly mixture that holds together when you press it. Grease a spring form cake tin (one that you can easily remove the base from) with coconut oil, then pour the crust mixture in and evenly spread it on the bottom and press it down firmly. Now put it in the fridge to chill while you make the filling.

Make some fresh coconut milk by blending the coconut meat or dried coconut with 3 cups of water and then straining the milk out. Then blend 2 cups of the coconut milk with the macadamia nuts, coconut oil, vanilla, lemon juice and salt until you produce a thick luscious cream.

Pour the cream into the crust, pop it in the fridge for 3 hours until its set or in the freezer for just over an hour. Once the cake is set, decorate with the mango, strawberries and kiwi and drizzle the passion fruit seeds all over it and enjoy!!!

Berry Cheesecake Bars

These handy little treats can be a delicious dessert, an afterschool snack for a lucky child or a between meals snack for a lucky, well, anyone actually!!! Makes about 8-12 bars.

For the crust you'll need:
2 cups of almonds
1 cup of desiccated coconut
1 cup of dates
A pinch of salt
2tbsp of coconut oil
For the topping you'll need:
1 ½ cups of fresh blueberries
1tbsp of honey or maple syrup

For the filling you'll need:
2 cups macadamia or cashew nuts soaked for 5hrs
½ cup maple syrup
¼ cup of lime juice
½ cup of melted coconut butter/oil
A pinch of salt
1 tsp vanilla extract or the seeds from 1 vanilla pod
1 cup of dried coconut or mature coconut meat
3 cups of water

You'll need to: First make the pie crust by putting all the crust ingredients in a food processor and processing until it becomes a crumbly mixture that holds together when you press it. Grease a square or rectangular (preferably) spring form cake tin (one that you can easily remove the base from) with coconut oil, then pour the crust mixture in and evenly spread it on the bottom and press it down firmly. Now put it in the fridge to chill while you make the filling.

Make some fresh coconut milk by blending the coconut meat or dried coconut with 3 cups of water and then straining the milk out. Then blend 2 cups of the coconut milk with the macadamia nuts, coconut oil, vanilla, lemon juice and salt until you produce a thick luscious cream.

Pour the cream into the crust, pop it in the fridge for 3 hours until its set or in the freezer for just over an hour. Once the cake is set, put half the blueberries in a food processor with the honey/maple syrup and briefly process to finely chop up the berries. Pour the chopped berries over the cheesecake layer, scatter with the remaining berries on top, return to the freezer for 30mins to become firm. Once it's firm, run a knife around the sides of it to remove it from the tin so you can more easily slice it into about 8-12 bars, serve and enjoy!!! Keep it in the fridge until ready to eat.

Chocolate Strawberry Cream Pie

This is the best raw chocolate sponge type cake I've tasted, which was inspired by Lisa Viger's book Raw On $10 a day of less. Serves 8-10.

You'll need:
2tbsp of maple syrup or honey
1 cup of buckwheat soaked for 5hrs
¼ cup of chocolate powder
½ cup ground flax soaked in 1 cup of water for 30mins
½ tsp of vanilla extract
A pinch of salt
I ripe banana
2tbsp of coconut oil
¾ cup of date soaked for 30mins (keep soaking water)
About 30 medium strawberries – I large punnet
1 cup of macadamia cream from page 52

You'll need to: Put the dates and ½ cup of the date soaking water into a food processor and process until smooth. Then add the buckwheat, maple syrup/honey, salt, vanilla, coconut oil, chocolate powder and flax and process again until fairly smooth, like a cooked cake batter. Then lightly grease a dehydrator sheet or baking paper with coconut oil, pour about 1 ½ cups or half the batter onto the sheet to make a circular cake base that's about ½ inch thick. Then repeat for the remaining cake batter to create 2 cakes in total. Dehydrate them for 3hrs on one side and then flip and do the other side for 3hrs or until spongy.

Next place one cake base on a plate, spread on half the cream and half the strawberries, then place the other cake on top of the strawberries, cover with the rest of the cream and the remaining strawberries. Ta-da!!!

Pumpkin Pie

I never had any success making a raw vegan pumpkin pie when I actually used pumpkins! But this version tasted just like a cooked pumpkin pie and was very simple to make, even though you do need to juice some carrots first. Serves 8-10.

For the crust you'll need:
2 cups of almonds
1 cup of desiccated coconut
1 cup of dates
A pinch of salt
2tbsp of coconut oil

For the filling you'll need:
2 cups of macadamia or cashew nuts soaked for 5hrs
½ cup of fresh carrot juice (about 3 medium carrots juiced)
¼ cup of maple syrup or honey
½ cup of coconut oil
½ tsp vanilla extract
1 ½ tsp of pumpkin pie or mixed spice or ½ tsp each of cinnamon, nutmeg & ginger

You'll need to: First make the pie crust by putting all the crust ingredients in a food processor and processing until it becomes a crumbly mixture that holds together when you press it. Grease a spring form cake tin (one that you can easily remove the base from) with coconut oil, then pour the crust mixture in and evenly spread it on the bottom and up the sides and press it down firmly to create a pie crust with sides that the filling can be poured into (see picture below). Now put it in the fridge to chill while you make the filling.

To make the filling, put all the filling ingredients into a blender and blend until smooth and creamy. Then pour the filling into the crust and put in the fridge to set for 2-3hrs or in the freezer for just over and hour or until firm. Then slice, serve and enjoy. Keep it in the fridge until ready to eat.

Mango Pie

You'll be amazed that the filling for this pie has just 2 ingredients and it tastes amazing. It's become a firm favourite of many friends, whether they normally like raw food or not. Serves 6-8

For the crust you'll need:
2 cups of almonds
1 cup of desiccated coconut
1 cup of dates
A pinch of salt
2tbsp of coconut oil
For the filling you'll need:
2 cups of dried mango soaked in 2 cups of water for 20mins
1/2 cup of fresh blueberries or raspberries to garnish

You'll need to: First make the pie crust by putting all the crust ingredients in a food processor and processing until it becomes a crumbly mixture that holds together when you press it. Grease a spring form cake tin (one that you can easily remove the base from) with coconut oil, then pour the crust mixture in and evenly spread it on the bottom and up the sides and press it down firmly to create a pie crust with sides that the filling can be poured into. Now put it in the fridge to chill while you make the filling.

To make the filling, simply put the soaked mangos and the water they've been soaked in, into a blender and blend until very smooth with no lumps. Pour into the pie crust, garnish with the berries and enjoy.

Here's one I made at a Leah's Raw Food Feast
Live Workshop just before we tucked into it ☺

Apple Crumble

A great substitute for the cooked version with very similar flavors for you to enjoy.
Serves 6.

You'll need:
8 apples (Braeburn, gala and jazz work well)
4tbsps of maple syrup or honey
½ cup of almonds
½ cup of walnuts soaked for 2hrs, drained, soaked for another 2hrs then dehydrated for 5hrs or overnight until dry – you can used unsoaked dry ones if you don't have a dehydrator
¼ cup of dates
¼ tsp salt
¼ tsp of mixed spice x 2
2tbsp of lime juice

You'll need to: Wash, peel, core and dice 5 apples and put them into a pie dish or serving bowl. Wash peel, core and chop up the other 3 apples and blend them with ¼tsp of mixed spice, lime juice and 2tbsp of honey or maple syrup to make an apple sauce. Pour the applesauce onto the chopped apple and stir thoroughly.

To make the crumble, put the almonds, walnuts, salt, dates, ¼ tsp mixed spice and coconut oil into a food processor and process until a crumble mixture is formed. Then simply sprinkle the crumble over the apples and enjoy.

Leah's Note: You can serve this with sweet macadamia cream on page 52 and you can put the whole thing in a dehydrator for 30mins or an oven on the lowest setting for 5mins to warm it very slightly.

Fruit Butterfly

This was one of the 'cakes' at my 1st & 3rd daughter's party one year and it was the first to go!!! Serve 4-6.

You'll need:
2 large mangos sliced
2 kiwis pealed and sliced
1 cup of strawberries sliced
½ cup of blueberries sliced in half

You'll need to: On a very large serving place, make the shape of a butterfly using the picture below as a guide.

Start making the body by laying the kiwi slices down the middle of the plate, slightly overlapping each other. Then make the top two wings by laying the sliced strawberries at the top 1/3 of the body on either side. Next make the two larger bottom wings by laying the mango slices either side of the remaining 2/3 of the body. You could reverse this so the top wings are large and the lower wings are smaller.

Lastly place 2 blueberries at the top of the body to make eyes, use about 9 on either side of the head to make the antennae and then 5 coming out of each of the bottom wings on either side to make the legs. Enjoy!

Chocolate Dipped Fruit Kebabs

This is a cleaner, healthier version of chocolate fondue or a chocolate fountain to form the centerpiece of any special party table. Serves 4.

You'll need:
2 cups of strawberries
3 bananas
4 kiwis
¼ cup of maple syrup / honey
¼ cup of raw chocolate powder
¼ cup of virgin coconut oil

You'll need to: Make the sauce by mixing the coconut oil, chocolate powder and maple syrup together in a bowl into a smooth sauce. If the coconut oil is at room temperature it should mix well, if not, it will quickly soften as you mix it vigorously.

Next prepare the fruit by washing, destalking and slicing the strawberries into quarters, peeling and quartering the kiwis and peeling and slicing the banana into chunks. Push the fruits pieces onto a kebab skewer or arrange them on a plate, put a small bowl of chocolate sauce on the plate with them and tuck in.

Leah's Note: You can use the chocolate sauce to drizzle over ice cream, muesli, pancakes, pies or anything you like really and any combination of fruit will work in this recipe too.

Apple Cinnamon Chips With Salted Caramel Dip

When my sister told me she just made a salted caramel sauce that was so good she wanted to bath in it, I knew it was time to get in the kitchen and create a raw version for this book and here it is. In a word, it's fantabulous, enjoy. Serves 2-3

For the salted caramel you'll need:
1/3 cup of honey or maple syrup
¼ cup of peanut, cashew or almond butter
A generous pinch of salt
For the apple cinnamon chips you'll need:
3 apples
1 level teaspoon of cinnamon
½ cup lemon juice or 1tsp of vitamin c powder (ascorbic acid) & 2 cups of water

You'll need to: Prepare the apples by either washing, quartering and coring them, then slice each quarter into slices about 1/4 – 1/3 inch thick or by slicing the whole apple into full circles. Then thoroughly mix the lemon juice or ascorbic acid powder into the 2cups of water and soak the apple slices in this mixture for 5mins. Lay the slices on a paper towel or clean kitchen towel and pat dry, then place them on a dehydrator tray, generously sprinkle with cinnamon and dehydrate for 8-12hrs or until they are completely dry, bendy and rubbery.

To make the salted caramel, simply put the honey/maple syrup, nut butter and salt in a bowl and mix it well until fully combined. If it is too thick to mix, add 1tsp of hot water at a time and keep mixing until it's the consistency you'd like.

Arrange the apple slices on a plate with a small bowl of the caramel sauce and eat by dipping the apple into the sauce or drizzle over the apples and enjoy!!!

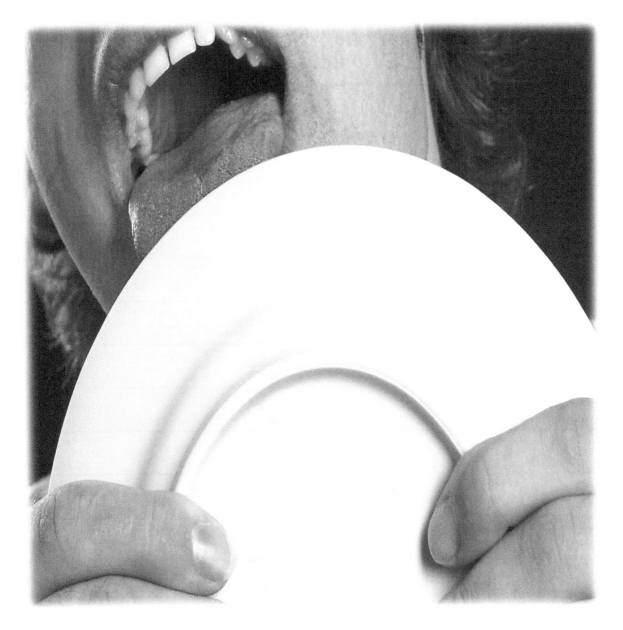

"Find healthy food that tastes great, so your mouth and body love your plate"

Leah Salmon

Your Recipe Notes

_____

_____

_____

_____

_____

_____

_____

_____

_____

_____

_____

_____

_____

_____

_____

_____

Success Meal Plans

To help you put all these recipes in some kind of a plan, which makes it easier for you to have a fantastic raw experience, here are 9 meal plans for you to choose from.

You can choose from

Plan 1: The Variety Meal Plan – Here you get to eat something different everyday for breakfast lunch and dinner, with a variety of desserts and drinks

Plan 2: The Double Day Meal Plan – For easier meal planning and to cut preparation time, you have one meal for dinner one day & again for lunch the next day. You also have the same breakfasts and drinks, snacks & desserts for 2 days in a row.

Plan 3: The High Raw Transition Meal Plan – For those who want to take it a bit slower, spend 9 days with mainly raw meals, but some cooked foods too.

Plan 4: The Carbohydrate Type Plan – Carbohydrate types have a lot of choice as raw vegans, but here's a plan with really high carbohydrates and lower proteins and fats, but definitely not fat free.

Plan 5: The Protein Type Plan – Protein Types can have a harder time on a raw vegan diet, so here are the highest protein and fat meals you can use to keep your levels up.

Plan 6: Juicy Plan – Don't have a dehydrator? No worries, this plan has you covered, with no recipes that need a dehydrator.

Plan 7: The Nutless Plan – If you have an allergy or intolerance to nuts, this plan is especially for you. None of the recipes have nuts in them, apart from coconut milk, which can be replaced with water in most cases.

Plan 8: The 5 Day Trial Run – Eat 100% raw diet for 5 days to prepare you for the 9 days.

Plan 9: The 3 Day Mini Taster – Spend 3 days 100% raw to wet your whistle a bit, before committing to 5 or 9 days.

Plan 1: The Variety Meal Plan

	Breakfast	Lunch	Dinner	Snack/Dessert/Drink
Day 1	Vanilla Chia Pudding	Tuna Salad	Creamy Green Soup	Green Smoothie
Day 2	Banana Split	Mushroom Walnut Burgers	Spaghetti & Sauce	Red Pepper Dip and Avocado fries
Day 3	Strawberry Pancakes & Cream	Tabouli	Humus Cabbage Wraps	Green Power Juice
Day 4	Muesli	Eggless Egg Salad	Spicy Sweetcorn Coleslaw	Hazelnut Hot Chocolate
Day 5	Melon Bowl	Walnut Burritos	Kale & Tomato Salad	Pinacolada
Day 6	Hi Enz	Plantain & Okra Stew	Courgette Avocado rolls	Sunflower Pate & Corn Chips
Day 7	Mango Avocado Pudding	Mushroom Soup	Bloomed Wild Rice Salad	Tahini Carob Milk
Day 8	Granola Berries & Cream	Nori Rolls	Easy Peasy Pizza	Spicy Lime and Avocado Dip with Cucumber & Carrot Sticks
Day 9	Spiced Buckwheat Porridge	Mango Salsa & Tomato Buckwheat Bread	Super Sprout Salad	Carrot Cake & Lemon Frosting

Plan 2: The Double Days Meal Plan

	Breakfast	Lunch	Dinner	Snack/ Dessert
Day 1	Hi Enz	Mushroom & Walnut Burgers	Super Sprout Salad & Corn Chips	Green Smoothie
Day 2	Hi Enz	Super Sprout Salad & Corn Chips	Tuna Salad	Green Smoothie
Day 3	Melon Bowl	Tuna Salad	Falafel & Pretty Salad	Apple Crumble
Day 4	Melon Bowl	Falafel & Pretty Salad	Tabouli & Spring Rolls	Apple Crumble
Day 5	Banana Nut Pudding	Tabouli & Spring Rolls	Butternut Squash & Tomato Soup	Flax Crackers & Chickpea Humus
Day 6	Banana Nut Pudding	Butternut Squash & Tomato Soup	Spaghetti & Sauce	Flax Crackers & Chickpea Humus
Day 7	Muesli	Spaghetti & Sauce	Coconut Curry Soup	Green Power Juice
Day 8	Muesli	Coconut curry Soup	Greens, beans & Rice	Green Power Juice
Day 9	Mango Avocado Pudding	Greens, beans & Rice	Humus Cabbages Wrap	Macaroons

Plan 3: The High Raw Transition Meal Plan

	Breakfast	Lunch	Dinner	Snack/Dessert /Drink
Day 1	Vanilla Chia Pudding	Cooked meal	Cooked meal	Green Smoothie
Day 2	Muesli	Cooked meal	Kale, Mango & Tomato Salad	Cooked snack /desert/ drink
Day 3	Vanilla Chia Pudding	Cooked meal	Kale, Mango & Tomato Salad	Cooked snack /desert/ drink
Day 4	Melon Bowl & Green Smoothie	Sweet Spicy Sweetcorn Coleslaw on romaine	Cooked meal	Chocolate Milk Shake
Day 5	Melon Bowl & Green Smoothie	Sweet Spicy Sweetcorn Coleslaw on romaine	Cooked meal	Green Power Juice
Day 6	Muesli	Tuna Salad on romaine	Cooked meal	Berry Cheesecake Bars
Day 7	Mango Avocado Pudding	Tuna Salad on romaine	Super Sprout Salad & Flax crackers	Berry Cheesecake Bars
Day 8	Hi Enz	Super Sprout Salad & Flax crackers	Nori Rolls	Carrot cake
Day 9	Strawberry Pancakes & Cream	Nori rolls	Eggless Egg salad	Carrot cake

Plan 4: The Carbohydrate Meal Plan

	Breakfast	Lunch	Dinner	Snack/Drink /Dessert
Day 1	Mango Shots & Berry Yoghurt Smoothie	Tabouli & Courgette Bread	Creamy Green Soup	Sunflower Pate & Carrot sticks
Day 2	Banana Split	Spring Rolls	Fruit & Veg Salad	Fuzzy Pink Lemonade
Day 3	Melon Bowl	Tabouli & Courgette Bread	Super Sprout Salad	Sunflower Pate & Carrot sticks
Day 4	Muesli (more fruit than nuts)	Super Sprout Salad	Curry Sauce on salad leaves & Veggie burgers	Green Power Juice
Day 5	Green Smoothie	Kale & Tomato Salad	Plantain & Okra Stew	Kale Chips & Cheese Sauce
Day 6	Spiced Buckwheat Porridge	Plantain & Okra Stew	Kale & Tomato Salad	Apple, Carrot & Celery Juice
Day 7	Melon Bowl	Fruit & Veg Salad	Butternut & Tomato Soup	Kale Chips & Cheese Sauce
Day 8	Granola, Berries & Cream	Creamy Green Soup	Kale, Mango & Tomato Salad	Pink Carrot Smoothie
Day 9	Mango Shots & Pinacolada	Butternut & Tomato Soup	Curry Sauce on salad leaves & Veggie burgers	Green Power Juice

Plan 5: The Protein Type Meal Plan

	Breakfast	Lunch	Dinner	Snack/Drinks /Dessert
Day 1	Muesli	Eggless Egg Salad	Humus Cabbage Wrap	Macaroons
Day 2	Mango Avocado Pudding	Bloomed Wild Rice Salad	Super Sprout Salad & Falafel	Halva & Green Power Juice
Day 3	Granola, Berries & Cream	Sweetcorn Coleslaw	Eggless Egg Salad	Berry Yoghurt Smoothie
Day 4	Hi Enz	Courgette & Avocado Rolls	Mushroom Soup	Tracker bar
Day 5	Banana Nut Pudding	Tuna Salad	Mushroom Walnut Burgers	Pumpkin Pie
Day 6	Vanilla Chia Pudding	Mushroom & Walnut Burgers	Greens, Beans & Rice	Walnut Fudge
Day 7	Granola Berries & Cream	Nori Rolls	Easy Pizza	Green Smoothie with 1tbsp coconut oil
Day 8	Hi Enz	Greens Beans & Rice	Courgette Avocado Rolls	Tahini Milk
Day 9	Mango Avocado Pudding	Nori Rolls	Mushroom Soup	Green Smoothie with 1tbsp coconut oil

Plan 6: The Juicy Plan

	Breakfast	Lunch	Dinner	Snack/Dessert /Drink
Day 1	Vanilla Chia Pudding	Tuna Salad	Creamy Green Soup	Green Smoothie
Day 2	Vanilla Chia Pudding	Walnut Burritos	Spaghetti & Sauce	Red Pepper Dip and carrot sticks
Day 3	Mango Avocado Pudding	Tabouli	Walnut Burritos	Green Power Juice
Day 4	Mango Avocado Pudding	Eggless Egg Salad	Sweet spicy Coleslaw	Hazelnut Hot Chocolate
Day 5	Muesli	Walnut Burritos	Kale & Tomato Salad	Pinacolada
Day 6	Hi Enz	Plantain & Okra Stew	Courgette Avocado rolls	Kefir
Day 7	Hi Enz	Mushroom Soup	Bloomed Wild Rice Salad	Fuzzy Pink Lemonade
Day 8	Granola Berries & Cream	Bloomed Wild Rice Salad	Easy Peasy Pizza	Spicy Lime and Avocado Dip with cucumber & carrot Sticks
Day 9	Banana Nut Pudding	Falafel & Super Sprout Salad	Nori Rolls	Carrot Cake & Lemon Frosting

Plan 7: The Nutless Plan

	Breakfast	Lunch	Dinner	Snack/Dessert /Drink
Day 1	Spiced Buckwheat Porridge (swap coconut milk for water)	Plantain & Okra Stew	Spaghetti & Pesto & Romaine	Green Power Juice
Day 2	Mango Shots & Peach Berry Smoothie	Buckwheat & Tomato Bread & Avocado Fries	Super Sprout Salad & Mango Salsa	Green Smoothie
Day 3	Melon Bowl	Plantain & Okra Stew	Spaghetti & Pesto & Romaine	Pink Carrot Smoothie
Day 4	Green Smoothie & Mango Shots	Nori Rolls & Salad	Kale, Mango & Tomato Salad	Red Power Juice
Day 5	Green Soup	Spring Rolls & Salad	Mushroom, Kale & Olive Pizza	Apple, Carrot & Celery Juice
Day 6	Vanilla Chia Pudding (swap coconut milk for water)	Mushroom, Kale & Olive Pizza	Corn Chips & Pretty Salad	Avocado Fries & Hot Sauce
Day 7	Spiced Buckwheat Porridge (swap coconut milk for water)	Butternut & Tomato Soup	Kale, Mango & Tomato Salad	Fuzzy Pink Lemonade

Plan 8: The 5 Day Trial Run Meal Plan

	Breakfast	Lunch	Dinner	Snack/Dessert
Day 1	Melon Bowl	Kale, Mango & Tomato Salad	Mushroom Walnut Burgers	Green Power Juice
Day 2	Granola Berries & Cream	Plantain & Okra Stew	Spring Rolls	Pink Ice Cream
Day 3	Hi Enz	Nori Rolls	Tabouli	Green Smoothie
Day 4	Mango Shots	Kale, Mango & Tomato Salad	Mango Salsa & Corn Chips	Chocolate Dipped Kebabs
Day 5	Strawberry Pancakes	Greens Beans & Rice	Creamy Green Soup	Halva

Plan 9: The 3 Day Mini Taster Meal Plan

	Breakfast	Lunch	Dinner	Snack/Dessert
Day 1	Strawberry Pancakes	Kale, Mango & Tomato Salad	Sweet Spicy Sweetcorn Coleslaw	Green Power Juice
Day 2	Hi Enz	Courgette Avocado Rolls	Tuna Salad	Green Smoothie
Day 3	Melon Bowl	Super Sprout Salad	Eggless Egg Salad	Berry Yoghurt Smoothie

Useful Links

www.rawfoodcoach.com
www.thegardendiet.com
www.detoxyourworld.com
www.therawtarian.com/raw-food-recipes
www.westonpricefoundation.org

Bibliography
Rawvolution by Matt Amsden
The Joy Of Living Live by Zakkah
The Best Of Raw Freedom Community by Carmella

About the Author
Leah Salmon – The Naturally You Coach

The Naturally You Coach, speaker, coach, bestselling author, founder of The Naturally You Day, editor of Naturally You magazine and natural health enthusiast, Leah has worked with people of all ages worldwide over the past 12 years, helping them to use their foods, natural remedies, lifestyle changes and their mindset to boost their health. More recently, Leah began to focus on helping busy parents professionals and business owners like herself to find time and motivation to achieve their health and life goals.

Her journey into natural health and nutrition began when she was just 11 years old when she decided to become vegetarian. Her stressful, soya and junk food filled teens resulted in her developing a concerning gynecological condition.

After seeking help from doctors who dismissed her condition, she began studying nutrition, aromatherapy and herbal medicine and managed to cure herself using herbs and foods. This sparked her passion to help others use the power of nature and coaching, as she had done, to free themselves of illness, so they don't need to suffer as she had done.

The biggest message that Leah wants to spread is that improving your health naturally, using whole natural foods is much easier than many people think, you don't have to put up with your health conditions or be bound to a life on medication to manage symptoms. Vibrant health is not found in a pill, surgery, harmful chemical or crash fad diet, but in living a life that's Naturally You. You can break free from disease, live a fulfilling and rich life and achieve your health goals and most importantly, with support, there's nothing you can't achieve.

Leah runs private & group coaching programs, has an active YouTube channel, a popular free ezine, home study courses (available on www.AmunUniversity.com) and currently has 6 bestselling books with more to come. She also has an annual natural health event called The Naturally You Day and a natural health and wellness magazine called Naturally You.

Also from Leah Salmon

"Becoming Naturally You – 39 Simple Steps To Naturally Transform Your Mind, Diet & Life!"

This is a simple program of 39 weekly small steps you can make to naturally improve your life and health naturally.

You can find Leah at:

Email	leah@thenaturallyyoucoach.com
Websites	www.TheNaturallyYouCoach.com
	www.AmunUniversity.com
Facebook (Profile page)	www.facebook.com/thenaturalyounetwork
Facebook (Fan Page)	www.facebook.com/leahthenaturallyyoucoach
Twitter	www.twitter.com/naturalyoucoach
You Tube	www.youtube.com/user/NaturallyYouCoach
Instagram	www.instagram.com/naturallyyoucoach
Pintrest	www.pinterest.com/naturalyoucoach/
LinkedIn	www.linkedin.com/in/leahsalmon

Lightning Source UK Ltd.
Milton Keynes UK
UKOW07f0153030616

275527UK00006B/10/P